Tests and Exams in Singapore Schools

What School Leaders, Teachers and Parents Need to Know

Tests and Exams in Singapore Schools

What School Leaders, Teachers and Parents Need to Know

Kaycheng SOH

WS Education

NEW JERSEY · LONDON · SINGAPORE · BEIJING · SHANGHAI · HONG KONG · TAIPEI · CHENNAI · TOKYO

Published by

WS Education, an imprint of
World Scientific Publishing Co. Pte. Ltd.
5 Toh Tuck Link, Singapore 596224
USA office: 27 Warren Street, Suite 401-402, Hackensack, NJ 07601
UK office: 57 Shelton Street, Covent Garden, London WC2H 9HE

National Library Board, Singapore Cataloguing in Publication Data
Name(s): Soh, Kaycheng.
Title: Tests and exams in Singapore schools : what school leaders, teachers and
    parents need to know / Kaycheng Soh.
Description: Singapore : WS Education, an imprint of World Scientific
    Publishing Co. Pte. Ltd., [2017]
Identifier(s): OCN 1001750450 | ISBN 978-981-32-2706-4 (paperback) |
    978-981-32-2705-7 (hardcover)
Subject(s): LCSH: Educational tests and measurements--Singapore. | Examinations--Singapore. |
    Schools--Singapore--Examinations.
Classification: DDC 371.262095957--dc23

British Library Cataloguing-in-Publication Data
A catalogue record for this book is available from the British Library.

Desk Editor: Shreya Gopi

Typeset by Stallion Press
Email: enquiries@stallionpress.com

Preface

School leaders, teachers, and parents share a common concern — their students' or children's performance in assessment. This means the three parties need shared knowledge of what assessment is and about for mutual understanding. In other words, they need to know about tests and exams so as to ensure that assessments are conducted professionally and the outcomes (in terms of test and exam results, usually) are interpreted in such a manner that does not give rise to unnecessary misunderstanding — which makes everyone concerned unhappy. On a positive note, knowledge of assessment enables the three parties to have mutual appreciation and even collaboration, all for the good of the central figure of schooling, the students/children.

While Singapore's education system is freeing up and becoming more flexible, thus providing more channels for individualized development, exams and tests are still important for various purposes. The high-stakes nature of exams and tests remains very much the same.

In this context, school leaders, teachers, and parents are naturally concerned about the students' academic performance throughout schooling. However, they need be better informed about exams and tests and related issues because misunderstanding about assessment can only create unnecessary misinterpretation and unwarranted worries.

This book is written with school leaders, teachers, and parents in mind with the view of helping them to better understand the processes and products of assessment (mainly through tests and exams). Because of the complex nature of assessment, some technical terms and statistical concepts are inevitable for a fuller appreciation of the pros and cons of some assessment practices. However, effort was consciously made to present them in as plain a language as possible and with examples and analogies. Hopefully, doing so makes such important knowledge more palatable.

It cannot be over-emphasized that exams and tests are a critical and even vital aspect of children's educational development. It is of such import that it demands better understanding on the part of three parties — they owe it to their children.

In the preparation of this book, references were made to relevant journal articles and other documents. However, these are not listed in the usual manner as the book is not meant to be an academic discourse but to share practical ideas with the readers. That said, interesting and useful websites are listed instead for readers who wish to follow up and do more in-depth reading.

KCS

About the Author

Dr. SOH Kay Cheng retired as a Senior Fellow of the Psychological Studies Academic Group at the National Institute of Education, Nanyang Technological University, Singapore. Currently, Dr. Soh is Research Consultant at the Singapore Centre for Chinese Language, Nanyang Technological University.

He obtained his Doctor of Philosophy (1985) from the National University of Singapore with his research on English-Chinese code-switching among Singapore children. Before this, he studied at the University of Manchester, United Kingdom, for his Master of Education (Educational Psychology) and Diploma in Educational Guidance in the years 1970 and 1965, respectively. In 2016, he was conferred as the first Senior Fellow of the Singapore Centre for Chinese Language for his contributions to research on Chinese Language teaching.

As a teacher educator and educational researcher, Dr. Soh joined the then Singapore Teachers' Training College in 1961 and worked in the Ministry of Education from 1975 and 1981. He was later the Principal of the Nanyang Academic of Fine Arts from 1994 to 1997.

Dr. Soh has a large number of publications, both locally and in Australia, Britain, Germany, Hong Kong, Japan, and the United States. Topics cover a wide range including language learning, creativity, world university ranking, grade-point-average, teacher research, etc., etc. He developed the *Creativity Fostering Teacher Behaviour Scale* (CFTIndex) in 2000 and it has been widely used by creativity researchers over the world, translated into Spanish, Turkish, and Chinese, and used as the main data collection instrument for some PhD dissertations. He has also published several books on education topics and action research, in Chinese and English.

His consultancy services include several Ministries in Singapore and the Hong Kong SAR Education Bureau and the Hong Kong Baptist University. He has been very active in community work and served on the National Arts Council Board, the Singapore Chinese Orchestra Board, and the Chinese Development Assistance Council Education Committee. He also served for two years as the Chairman of the Government's Feedback Group (Education). In recent years, he serves as a consultant training the Research Activists at the Ministry of Education and is the chief editor of its publication *North Star: A Publication for Educational Practitioners.* Moreover, Dr. Soh has been conducting action research workshops in many Singapore schools.

Contents

Preface   v

About the Author   vii

1. What Do We Need to Know About Tests and Exams?   1

    Weight watching and exam   1
    Assessment, tests, and exams   3
    Questions to ask   4

2. Why Must Students Take Exams?   7

    Feedback and motivation   7
    Diagnosis and remedy   9
    Classification and guidance   11

3. What Makes a Fair Exam?   15

    A fair scale   15
    A fair question   16
    Facility and discrimination   16
    Proper coverage   18
    Beyond the textbook   20

4. Answers Students Have to Choose   23

    MCQ   24
    True-false   27
    Matching   28

5. Answers Students Have to Write   31
    Fill-in-the-blank   31
    Short-answer questions   35
    Essay-type questions   37

6. T-score: What Is It, and Why?   43
    Same marks, different meanings   44
    Some simple stats   48
    Equals are not equivalents   49
    The normal curve   50

7. What Is a Good Mark?   53
    Passing marks   53
    A good mark   55
    Improvement?   56

8. Can Exams be Trusted?   59
    Reliability   59
    Validity   63
    Biases   65
    Consequences   68
    Why some bright children do not do well?   70
    Relation between reliability and validity   72

9. Preparing for Exams and Coping with Exam Stress   73
    Exam anxiety   74
    Signs of exam anxiety   76
    Anxiety and achievement   77
    Preparing for exams physically and emotionally   78
    Preparing the student mentally   79
    Assessment Preparedness Scale   82

10. How Is Creativity Assessed?   85
    What is a creativity product?   85
    What are creative processes?   87
    Creative person   89
    Personal and cultural creativity   91
    How is creativity to be assessed?   92
    Creative Behaviour Scale   96

11. Project Work: What Is It For and How Is It Assessed?   99

What is project work?   99
Assessment of project work   101
What else can be considered?   105
Reconciling assessment disparity   107
Concluding remarks   109

12. Rubrics and *Assessment for Learning*   111

Why *assessment for learning?*   111
What is an assessment rubric?   112
Use of rubrics   115
Rubric scores   116
Reliability and validity of rubric assessment   118
Concluding remarks   119

13. Above-level Testing: Good or Bad?   121

Out-of-level testing (OLT) in the United States   121
Above-level testing in Singapore   122
Assumed benefits   122
Undesirable consequences   123
False information   125
The way ahead   127
Conclusion   128

14. Grade Point Average: Beware of Its Pitfalls   129

How is GPA calculated?   129
How did GPA come about?   130
What then are problems with GPA?   131
Conclusion   134
References   135

15. What Is Assessment Literacy?   137

Importance of assessment literacy   137
Measuring assessment literacy   139
Singapore context   141
Domains of assessment literacy   141
Concluding note   143

16. How Assessment Literate Are You?   145
   Assessment Literacy Scale   146
   Subtest 1: Nature and Function of Assessment   146
   Subtest 2: Design and Use of Test Items   147
   Subtest 3: Interpretation of Test Results   149
   Subtest 4: Reliability, Validity and Basic Statistics   150
   Answer Sheet   152
   Answer Keys   152
   Scores and Interpretation   153

Endnote   155

Appendix A: Statistical Concepts Plainly Explained   157

Appendix B: Interesting and Useful Websites   169

1. What Do We Need to Know About Tests and Exams?

Weight watching and exam

Are you a weight watcher? If you are, you are likely to do this frequently if not everyday. You step on a bathroom scale with minimum clothing on. Look at where the pointer stops and read the dial. Then, you compare the reading with a number that is in your mind all the time, say, 65kg. Now you find your weights somewhat higher than *that* number. Here, you conclude that you have an extra baggage to get rid of. So, you decide that you should go to the gym more often and should be resistant to the tempting *roti prata*, fried chicken, pizza, burger, French fries and, above all, sweetened canned drinks. (Incidentally, French fries have nothing to do with France.)

What has all this to do with exams (and tests, of course, but we will use *exam* for both)? First, the bathroom scale is a standard instrument for assessing your body weight, analogous to an *exam* or a *test* for assessing your children's learning.

Next, the pointer moves a distance from zero according to the force your body weight exerts on the spring inside the bathroom scale and it gives you the magic number. This is *measurement*, that is, assigning numbers according to rules (e.g., the heavier the weight, the higher the number). An exam also has its rules for awarding marks (scores) — more correct answers bring more marks.

Then, you compare the number shown on the dial with the number you have in mind. Where do you get this number? Of course, you get it from your family doctor, your health advisor or, more likely, a chart found in a health magazine. This number represents the ideal weight you should try to attain. The number takes into account your body frame, sex, and age; that's why there are several tables and you should refer to the correct one for you. This ideal number serves as a *standard* against which you compare your actual weight. By the way, most such tables are based on Westerners' physical conditions and may not be correct for us Asians.

When you compare your actual weight with the ideal weight, you are in fact comparing with a large number of people of similar body frame, sex, and age whose information was used to compile the tables, called *norms*. And, the norm is the standard. It helps you decide whether you are of the correct weight. This in fact is the *assessment*, judging the goodness-of-fit of your bodily health.

What happens, then, when your child takes an exam? When your child takes an exam, he is being measured by the test paper (a standard tool like the bathroom scale) common to all other children taking the same exam. He is then given a mark according to the marking scheme (rules) and the mark is supposed to show his ability in answering the questions that make up the exam.

Your child's score shows where he stands on the possible scale (say, from 0 to 100) and whether he has reached the expected standard set by the teacher. In Singapore schools, the convention is to take 50% of the possible maximum score as the passing mark which represents an acceptable performance in the various subjects.

Here, a peculiar thing needs be pointed out. All bathroom scales are built to measure weight in the same way. When you stand on different scales, you will get very much the same reading. This is not true of school exams. Since exam papers for different subjects and levels are based on different topics, a passing mark of 50% for different exams does not represent the same abilities and does not have the same meaning. For example, a 50% for English is not the same as a 50% for Math! (We will talk more about this later.)

By aligning the processes of weight watching and school exam, we can see clearly the complexity of such seemingly simple things. Each of these obviously involves several steps:

Weight watching	Action	School exam
Bathroom scale	Designing standard instrument	Teacher prepares exam papers
Stepping on the scale	Testing or examining	Students respond to the exam paper
Reading the dial for a number	Applying measurement	Teacher marks paper and assign marks
Compare the number with an ideal one (standard, norm)	Making comparison	Teacher/student/parent checks the mark against the passing mark
Decide whether the weight is 'correct'	Assessment	Teacher/student/parent concludes pass/fail
More exercise, less fattening food	Taking follow-up actions	Student do more study, remedial lessons

Assessment, tests, and exams

Armed with these ideas, we are now ready to take a closer look at the nature of exams and the role they play in your children' lives.

Exams (this includes all forms of tests) play a vital role in children's education in many countries, all the more so in Singapore where *high-stakes* exams have a critical and decisive effect on children's psychological well-being, educational development, and ultimately their life chances.

Parents are naturally highly anxious about the results their children get for the long series of assessment in school. There are first the weekly or fortnightly tests (which are exams in fact), and then the semester assessments (which are exams in reality but called by another name). The mid-year exams (now, a spade is called a spade) and the end-of-year exams are not to be missed.

A *test* covers fewer topics but in greater detail and the results children get may and may not be counted toward total marks at the end of the year.

This depends on the individual schools' policies. A *semester assessment* covers more topics than a weekly test does, and the results may contribute a certain percent to the final results. Of course, mid-year and end-of-year *exams* are supposed to cover a wider range of topics. The results of these exams are most important because they make up the largest percent of the final results that have a decisive effect on children's future development within the system.

According to this Singaporean usage, *test* is supposed to be less formal and less important; *assessment* a bit more formal and more important; and *exam* most formal and most important. Due to the long-term consequences of the high-stakes nature of results, even a supposedly more user-friendly term like *test* is equally threatening as the formidably sounding term like *exam* (perhaps, less so to young children who take the test/assessment/exam).

Whichever terms are used, they have one common element. They all use tests (the papers printed with a series of questions) which are standard or uniform procedures for assessing children's ability in doing something they are expected to be able to do. Thus, *tests* and *assessments* and *exams* actually refer to the one and same procedure of getting children to answer questions to show what they have learned, can do and do know. Hence, to avoid unnecessarily loading your mind and to simplify the discussion, *exams* will be used interchangeably with *tests* and *assessments* here and there in this book. They are standard procedures and they may and may not have anything to do with the standard to be achieved. Being *standard* here simply means that all children taking the same test must try to answer the same questions (although choices may be allowed sometimes in, say, essay writing), take the test at the same time, and are given the same amount of time to complete it.

Questions to ask

Against this background, there are a number of more specific issues to which parents may be oblivious. Some of the issues are:

1. What do we need to know about exams?
2. Why must students take exams?
3. What makes a fair exam?

4. Answers students have to choose
5. Answers students have to write
6. T-score: What is it, and why?
7. What is a good mark?
8. Can exams be trusted?
9. Preparing for exams and coping with exam stress
10. How is creativity assessed?
11. Project work: What for and how assessed?
12. Rubrics and assessment *for* learning
13. Above-level testing: Good or bad?
14. What is assessment literacy?
15. How assessment literate are you?

These are all very relevant and practical issues on which concerned parents, teachers, and school leaders need to be better informed. Equipped with such information, they can then better help the children in learning and preparing for exams, can see the children's performance in a more appropriate perspective, and will understand and accept the imperfection inherent in the educational assessment. All these will make them better parents, teachers, and school leaders in striving toward the goal of maximizing the benefits of educating their children.

2. Why Must Students Take Exams?

To many parents, teachers, and school leaders, exams serve only one purpose — checking whether their children are doing OK in schoolwork. Actually, there is much more to it. Let's go back to weight watching.

Feedback and motivation

When you get a reading of your body weight, it tells you whether you are of the correct weight for your body frame, sex, and age. This information is useful as feedback to you if you are on a slimming regime by being careful about what you put into your mouth and what you do to get rid of the excess flesh around the waist. In short, the information tells if you are on the right track on your way to better health and what you need to do next.

Likewise, when a student takes an exam, the mark he gets tells how well he fares in his learning. If he is concerned with his learning and performance (many children are not!), the very first question that comes to his mind may be *Have I passed? Have I reached my mother's expectation (100%)?* And, by looking into the exam paper marked by the teacher, he knows where he has done well and where he has not. Thus, exam provides *feedback* just like the information you get from the bathroom scale about your weight.

In the early years of psychology of learning, psychologists found that feedback was very important for effective learning. In their experiments, university students were to learn by hitting a target, blindfolded. They were seated in front of a blackboard (no white boards in those days), blindfolded, and were asked to throw a ball to hit a circle on the blackboard. He tried, tried, and tried without any perceivable improvement: *practice does NOT make perfect!*

Then, the psychologist began to give feedback by telling how far the ball was off-target and in which direction it should move. Lo and behold, the performance began to show improvement. The experiments showed that blind or aimless practice did not bring about better performance and feedback was needed to improve learning. By the way, most children do not see the purpose of repetitive practice they are asked to do (like doing the 'assessment books'), but they just do it to please their teachers and parents.

Closely related to feedback is *motivation*. Motivation means to *move*. Children are expected to move in the direction expected by the teachers. Very often, teachers use exam results to *move* (and not infrequently *push*) their students to study by setting a target, expecting students to get beyond a certain mark. Of course, how high the target is depends on the ambition. Most expect more marks, many expect perfect marks, and some do not bother. Thus, exam results become a tool to make children learn. Thus, to children who have been trained to become concerned with exams, getting high marks is a way of pleasing teachers and parents and getting rewards or, conversely, avoiding reprimands, deprivation, and punishment.

Psychologists talk about two types of motivation — *intrinsic* and *extrinsic*. Intrinsic motivation is the desire to learn because the activities are enjoyable and indeed enjoyed. For such activities, no incentives other than the opportunity to be engaged in the activities are needed to sustain the children's interest. In short, they do the activities to enjoy doing them. For example, a boy who plays with his train tracks finds it enjoyable for reasons only he knows, or he may not even know why he enjoys doing it. He continues to play for a long time, always to the displeasure of his mother who believes he should spent time more 'usefully', that is, doing school work. Unfortunately, much of schoolwork is not intrinsically enjoyable. Because of this, teachers try hard to think of ways and means to make schoolwork enjoyable, for example, disguising them as games. Because of this, parents, who have not been trained professionally, always resort to inducements such as promising rewards of all kind, from a coveted train set to a trip to Disneyland, or punishment, or both.

Thus, intrinsic motivation is replaced by extrinsic motivation. What is originally interesting and enjoyable to children become what they must do to get something else which may be attractive to them.

Extrinsic motivation is not bad in itself, if it works. It gives children a reason to learn things they do not normally enjoy learning. In this case, learning is not for enjoyment but for getting rewards or avoiding punishment; but, in the end, what needs to be learned is learned, and this is most important to parents (and, of course, teachers). One problem of extrinsic motivation is that, as research shows, when there is no incentive coming, learning will not happen. Worse, the strength of such extrinsic incentive needs be increased as time passes by, because something attractive enough earlier becomes less attractive later and thus loses its motivating power. The toys and the trips promised will have to become more and more expensive, a bigger train set or Disneyland in Tokyo and later the US. [1]

Another problem with extrinsic motivation is the loss of interest in what is originally interesting. In a series of experiments, children who enjoyed doing certain things (for instance, drawing colourful pictures, writing own stories) were given rewards ("prizes") for what they have done. When repeated often, they lost interest in the activities and craved for the rewards instead, and the quality of their creations deteriorated when rewards were not forthcoming. It seems that the originally interest in doing something was transferred to the rewards, and the activities lose their original attractiveness.

Diagnosis and remedy

If you are watching your weight under professional guidance, the health professional needs to know the progress you are making. More than this, she needs to modify the slimming programme where indicated. This means she should be able to pinpoint where more effective ways of weight control is needed.

Likewise, a student's learning is a complex undertaking. There are many things to recognize, to remember, to understand, and to apply. Learning in school looks simple to adults but, in fact, it is not as simple as adults always imagine! Depending on his motivation and ability, the child may have learned well some parts of what he has to learn and missed some other parts. And, in a typical class of 30 children, different children have different parts not learning well, although there may be some common errors.

How is a teacher to find out which are the parts children do not learn well? Of course, by assessment. After marking a set of test papers, the teacher will have a pretty good idea of where her class has done well and where it has not. Those parts that have not been learned well or not learned at all signal to her the need for remedial teaching to make good the deficit.

Remedial teaching depends on diagnosis of learning difficulties that show up as wrong answers in the assessment. For instance, the students may give wrong answers to a subtraction problem for several different reasons. Some boys gave wrong answers because they forgot to take away *one* from the number from which a 'borrowing' (renaming) was done. Other boys took the larger number below and minus from it the smaller number above. Other reasons were possible. The teacher's job is to find out from the results what the common causes of errors were. Following this, she would have to re-teach those concepts again and explain why some answers were wrong. In short, remedial teaching requires diagnosis of learning difficulties and these are based on what children do not do correctly.

Many schools conduct the so-called *remedial classes* in the afternoon or during vacation, with the intention to help children do better in exams. This is a noble gesture, as teachers are spending extra hours beyond their normal teaching loads. There are two things which need to be mentioned. First, calling such classes 'remedial' is a misnomer, because they are in most cases just extra time to go through what has been taught in the morning or during term time; it is basically a revision with additional practice. Thus, it is not remedial teaching is the real sense, because it is not necessarily based on diagnosis of learning difficulties, unless it is assumed that all children in the class have learned nothing or have the same problems, in the morning or during term time.

Secondly, the prevalence of such remedial classes gives rise to a host of questions: Could the teaching in the morning or during term time be made more effective so that such remedial classes are not needed? Effective teaching in the first round will reduce the need for subsequent second operation. Next, are they needed because the syllabuses are too demanding or overloaded, and if so, what could be done? While it is good to challenge the young minds, it is also necessary to bear in mind that certain concepts, by virtue of their complexity, can be learned only when the children have the prerequisites and are mentally mature enough.

This is where the Russian psychologist Leo S. Vygotsky's principle of *zone of proximal development* is good counsel — children learn best when the learning task is just a little more difficult than his current ability and he can master it by just putting in a little more effort. In other words, when the learning tasks are far above the head of the children, they cannot learn and will not learn, and frustration builds up such that they lose confidence and interest in learning.

The next question is simple. If such remedial classes are merely extra time beyond the stipulated curriculum time, call them *extra classes* so that nobody is misled to the erroneous impression that the schools and teachers have done such a poor job that remedies are extensively needed.

Classification and guidance

Singapore has a highly competitive education system that classifies children at a young age. We have the optional Primary Four Streaming Exercise. We have the Primary (Six) School Leaving Exam. We have the Secondary Four/Five General Certificate of Education (Ordinary Level), and we have the pre-university General Certificate of Education (Advanced Level). After each of these checkpoints, children move into a stream or track that is believed to best suit him.

There are people who believe that such classification is good and therefore necessary. There are others who point out the problems inherent in such a system. This is an issue beyond the scope of this book. Take the system as a given, the required classification needs information of the students' performance in the examined subjects. Such information is needed for making decisions regarding the movements of the students. Generally, students who have attained a specified level are deemed capable of benefiting from schooling at the next higher level, and are therefore channelled to streams or tracks believed to be most suitable to them. Because of such 'points of no return', exams become high-stake.

How trustworthy the exam results are in providing information for the classification of children touches on two important qualities of exam results (marks or grades) — their *reliability* and *validity* (which will be discussed subsequently). At this point, we have to have faith in the information and acknowledge that, disregarding reliability and validity, without such information, the decision of students' movement cannot be made. Hence, students need be assessed. This is, of course, the administrative function of assessment.

Besides the administrative use, assessment has a guidance function. This is the function that is partly administrative and partly professional. This function also overlaps to some extent with the functions of diagnosis and remedy.

Children who are extremely strong in the core subjects (that is, Languages, Math, and Science) may need special treatment such as the Gifted Education Programme that is specially design to meet the cognitive needs of the very intelligent children. Without such special programmes, very bright children will find schooling very boring, meaningless, and unchallenging. At the same time, precious human resource will be under-developed and, to Singapore, developing human capital is vital to national survival. To identify such children who need and qualify for special treatment, exam results provide the critically needed information.

On the other hand, there are children who, for some reasons, are rather slow in learning when compared with the general run of children of the same age. These children need early identification and intervention so that they are better equipped to cope with learning tasks designed for the so-called average children. Again, for maximizing the limited human resource that we have in Singapore, this group of children needs a different kind of special treatment. Learning support programmes are in place in schools to help them. Here, exam results are vital for correctly identifying who such children are. American experience shows that such special programme has long-term benefits that may not be obvious to people who take a short-term view of schooling.

In an American research, children from lower-income families were enrolled in the Head Start Project. In this project, children were given pre-skills training and were taken to places of cultural significance as well. In short, these children had the benefits of a well-designed curriculum that afforded them opportunities to learn what they normally did not have a chance to come across. The researchers followed up these children to the time when they were young adults of around 30 years of age. What then have been found? When compared with those of similar home background but were not in the project, the project children (now, young adults) had higher rates of university education, house ownership, higher average income, higher job positions, more outstanding achievements, and less marital problems and criminal offences. By contrast, the other group had a higher rate of school dropout, crime, divorce, and job loss. [2]

Thus, seen from various perspectives of children (and their parents), teachers, and school leaders, assessment is essential in that it examines the children's learning, progress, strengths, and problems. Without such information, many of the important functions performed by the school cannot be done. Assessment is necessary, although some may say, a necessary evil.

3. What Makes a Fair Exam?

Nobody will disagree that exams ought to be fair. But, what do we mean by *fair*? To answer, we need to go back to our analogy of weight watching.

A fair scale

Imagine that you have just bought a bathroom scale that has a very soft spring. Imagine also that you and some friends want to find out each other's body weight. Imagine further that regardless of who steps on the scale, it shows the same maximum reading, although it is obvious that some of you are much heavier than the others. If you like, imagine the opposite — whoever steps on the scale, the hand does not move at all because the scale has a very hard spring.

In both these unlikely situations, what information do you get? Nothing, except that you know the scale does not work correctly. Thus, you cannot tell from the readings the body weights you and your friends are interested to know. More damaging than this is that the scale does not tell who is heavier and who lighter. It gives 'equal treatment' to all. Is this fair?

In short, a fair bathroom scale ought to give information of the individuals' body weights and show the differences among the individuals. When the spring of the scale is too soft, the weights will be overestimated and this gives the wrong impression that you and all your friends are overweight. On the other hand, if the spring is too hard, all your weights are underestimated. More disappointing is that the weights you get do not reflect what you see obviously among yourselves in terms of the individual's body frame, height, and size.

Technically, we say that the scale does not have the proper *facility* (i.e., not responding to body weight correctly) and does not effectively *discriminate* (i.e., not making a difference between a lighter and a heavier person). Something like this can happen with an unfair exam, being either too easy or too demanding, and therefore do not accurately differentiate between more able and less able children.

A fair question

Imagine that a test has only one multiple-choice question (MCQ). This is a most unlikely situation in the real world, of course. To simplify our discussion, just imagine that there is such one-question exam.

A large group of children are most unlikely to have the same ability tested by the one-MCQ assessment. Now, they all take the test and all get the correct answer (called the *key*). With this information, can you tell who are able and who are unable, or who knows and who does not know the answer? Of course not. The opposite can also be true. When the whole group of children chose the wrong answers (called *distracters*), there is no information that can help you separate the sheep from the goats.

In other words, such one-item exam gives misleading information. It makes us mistakenly think that the whole group of children are capable (or incapable) in responding correctly to that one MCQ. To be realistic, imagine a test made up of some 30 such items and they all behave like the one item we have just talked about. This exam is useless in that it gives us no information about the children's individual ability.

What then should a fair exam paper with many questions be? Simply said, the individual questions, as well as the exam as a whole, should be neither too easy nor too difficult for the intended group of children. Technically speaking, we expect a fair exam (and the questions making up the paper) to have a *moderate facility* and show *acceptable discrimination*. And what's that?

Facility and discrimination

A few examples will make the concepts of *facility* (F) and *discrimination* (D) clear. In the table below, the first item is answered correctly by all

50 children in the high-total group and none from the low-total group, so F is 50(%) [(50 + 0)/100] and D is 1.00 [(50 − 0)/50]. This is an ideal item which is unlikely to be found in reality.

The second item is answered correctly by none of the highs but all of the lows, so F is also 50% [(0 + 50)/100] but D is −1.00 [(0 − 50)/50]. This is a horrible item which functions in the wrong way totally; it is also unlikely in reality.

The two items are used to illustrate the concepts. In reality, items fall between these extremes. Take the third item, 35 of the 50 highs get it right and only 10 of the lows do so. In other words, 70% highs are able to answer correctly and 20% of lows do likewise, so the total number of children answering correctly is 45 children out of 100, then F is 45% [(35 + 10)/100]. At the same time, D is 0.50 [(35 − 10)/50]. This item has a suitable F indicating that it is neither too easy for the children nor is it too difficult — an item of average difficulty (facility). The goodness of this item is that more highs than lows get it right, giving a D of 0.50, showing its power to differentiate between the highs and lows.

Item	Highs (N = 50)	Lows (N = 50)	F	D
1	50 (100%)	0 (0%)	50	1.00
2	0 (0%)	100 (0%)	50	−1.00
3	35 (70%)	10 (20%)	45	0.50

By convention, a question that has F between 41–60% answering correctly is a good item with moderate facility. Beyond this, a question with 61–80% correct response is considered as somewhat easy (high facility), and 81–100% means too easy (very high facility). On the other hand, a question answered correctly by 21–40% is difficult (low facility) and one by only 0 − 20% is too difficult (very low facility).

By convention also, a question that has D of 0.21 and above is considered as showing acceptable discrimination. Of course, the higher the D the better it is in that it is 'powerful' in separating the more able and less able students.

In practice, an exam should have items which have a wide range of F's so that there are some easy items, some difficult items, and mostly moderate items, but all the items must have acceptable D's (0.2 and above). Such an exam will be fair in that it is of moderate difficulty, neither does it penalize the weak children nor inflate the scores for all students. And, at the same time, it has sufficient discrimination power to differentiate between students of different ability.

Proper coverage

Given that an exam is made up of questions that have adequate facilities and discrimination, there remains an important question: How well does the exam reflect the topics stipulated in a syllabus?

A syllabus specifies the topics to be covered in terms of knowledge, skills, understanding, and the ability to apply the knowledge and skills. There are topics that are much more complex and hence more demanding in time and effort of the teacher and students. Even within a particular topic, not all knowledge, skills, and understanding are of equal importance. Normally, those more important ones will take up more time and effort of both the teacher and students.

Thus, an exam should reflect or be consistent with such differential importance. Moreover, at different stages of teaching a topic, the objectives may be different. At the beginning, it is more important that children learn the basic concepts and specific terms. At a later stage, it is more important that the children apply what they have learned to answer questions or solve problems not used in the lesson when it was taught. Thus, the same topic may have to be treated one way for weekly assessment and another for mid-year or year-end exams.

As things get more complicated, there is a need for a method to ensure such concordance between teaching and assessment. The method found to be helpful is the *Table of Specifications* (TOS). A TOS, also called a test-blueprint, is a two-dimension table. Normally, the topics or sub-topics are listed at the leftmost column of the table, and the levels of learning (for instance, recall, understanding, and application) are listed across the top row. Thus, many boxes are made by crossing topics (sub-topics) and levels of learning. In each of these boxes, a number indicate how many questions or marks are allocated to a particular sub-topic with a particular ability. In this way, a TOS maps how questions of a test are distributed among the sub-topics and levels of learning. It is like what an architect does when planning a building, hence *blueprint*. Sometimes, when other types of questions more than MCQs are used, the TOS boxes may also indicate the types of questions to be set. A typical TOS looks like this:

	Knowledge			Comprehension	Application	No. of items	% marks
	Terms	Symbols	Facts	Influence	Map reading		
Air pressure	1	2	2	4	3	12	20
Wind	1	2	2	11	2	18	30
Temperature	1	1	2	4	2	10	17
Humidity	1	2	1	5	5	14	23
Clouds	2	2	2	—	—	6	10
No. of items	6	9	9	24	12	60	—
% marks	**10**	**15**	**15**	**40**	**20**	—	**100**

By looking at the percentages at the bottom row, we can tell where the emphases are where levels of learning are concerned. In this example, obviously, the teacher places much greater emphasis on comprehension, followed by application, and not as much on knowledge. Similarly, by looking at the last column, it is clear that the topic *Wind* is given greater emphasis, followed by *Humidity*, and then Air *pressure*, etc.

Of course, where the emphasis is to be placed depends on the teacher's professional judgment on the nature of the topics and the kind of thinking. Needless to say, this is where great minds may not think alike — not all teachers will think in the same way when they set an exam like this. Their professional training, teaching experience, personal perception and preference play a significant part in making such a decision. This is where the fairness of an exam may be called to question.

It is not necessary that all topics or sub-topics are covered in an exam. An exam may concentrate on selected topics or sub-topics. Whichever way, the TOS should, however, reflect the emphases that have been placed during teaching as well as the relative importance of the topics in the context of the subject. When more questions and marks are given to topics (and sub-topics) that have not been given much emphasis in teaching, children are not fairly assessed. When more questions and marks are assigned to less important topic (or sub-topics), the exam is not assessing what subject matter experts deem essential.

In short, an exam is fair when it is designed in such a way that it reflects the emphasis given during teaching and the emphasis on important topics or sub-topics.

Beyond the textbook

Is it fair to examine children beyond what they have been taught? This is a rather tricky question.

Children (and their parents) are not happy that a test includes questions on knowledge, skills, and understanding not taught in class because this includes questions beyond the textbook. A classic example is the Mathematics question which asked for the second last digit of the sum of 1 to 100. It led to a hue and cry from the parents because they saw this as an unfair question. It is interesting that this problem is similar to the one of a young primary school boy by the name of Johann Carl Friedrich Gauss (1777–1855) who solved it within seconds when posed by his teacher to keep the class busy and quiet. Gauss later became a world famous mathematician whose name is always associated with the equally world famous Normal Curve or the *Gaussian distribution curve*.

When a teacher teaches, she aims at making sure that her children are able to understand and remember what she has taught them. When assessing, she should look for evidence that children are able to use the knowledge and skills in new situations, that is, able to *apply* what they have learned to answer unfamiliar questions and solve problems unseen before. This, the psychologists call *transfer of training*. And, the whole idea of education is based on this concept. If children are able to solve only those problems the solutions of which they have seen before, no education takes place!

When children can remember what has been taught them and can do nothing else with what they have learned, they have not learned! Take a simple example. What if a boy is able to recognize words in a language textbook only when the words appear in the original text but unable to recognize them when found on signboards, in newspapers, and many other print materials he comes across in his daily life? He can remember, yes, but has he learned? This is not only true of language learning but also of the learning of other subjects.

Here, you may need to learn about the difference between an *attainment test* and a *proficiency test*. An attainment test is normally based on a specific textbook and assesses only those that go into it. In contrast, a proficiency test goes beyond the textbook to assess the ability to use what has been learned to solve unfamiliar or unseen problems. Generally speaking, the former emphasizes recall and the latter understanding and application. In this sense, all tests should be proficiency tests, because schooling allows children to learn some knowledge, skills, and understanding which are believed to be important in their daily lives and beyond the classroom. In other words, education is based on the concept and possibility of transfer of training. Without transfer of training, schooling serves no useful purposes except keeping the school leaders, teachers, and students (and their parents) very busy.

Supposedly, the out-of-syllabus Mathematics question was meant to give some students good in Math an opportunity to show their capability to formulate their own solution. It would add on to the discrimination power of the paper by stretching the marks so that mathematically endowed children can be identified when necessary. In this sense, the question is a good one for a *proficiency* test of mathematical ability, although it may be an unfair question in an *attainment* test.

In highly selective exams for special purposes (e.g., tests used for scholarship selection), most or even all questions will be of this challenging type. In international competitions such as the Math Olympiad, questions are of this type, too. These are exams for special target groups for special purposes. As for the general run of children for general assessment purposes, more emphasis on attainment-type questions are appropriate, but should not totally exclude proficiency-type questions. Otherwise, able children are not given the chance they deserve to show their capabilities. And, the worse is that rote-learning and regurgitation are inadvertently encouraged.

So, we should accept exams that go beyond the textbooks, provided they do not go too far beyond. If your children are taking a scholarship exam or taking part in Math Olympiad or the like, it is a different matter altogether.

4. Answers Students Have to Choose

Do you realize that there are several types of weighing devices? Smaller than your bathroom scale is the scale in the Chemistry lab for weighing very small quantities of chemicals. There is even a smaller one for weighing diamonds. Don't forget the old-fashioned *tachin* made up of a calibrated stick and a plate hanging at one end and a movable weight hanging somewhere on the stick. You still see this in Chinese herbal medicine stores. On the other hand, you have the giant weighing machine with a large platform found in Changi Airport years back. Perhaps, they are still using it at warehouses for bulky and heavy bags of rice. Thus, you need different scales for different purposes.

There are several commonly used question types: the MCQ or multiple-choice questions, the T/F or true-false items, the matching items, the FIB or fill-in-the-blank items, the incomplete sentences, the SA or short-answer items, and, of course, the true essay questions that require extensive writing. These are like the different kinds of hand tools that fill a tool box — the screwdriver, the hammer, the spanner, wire-cutter, etc. Just as a DIY man needs these different tools to do different jobs, teachers need different types of questions to assess different learning outcomes.

You may also want to know that, in spite of the variety, there are actually only two broad types of questions. First, we have questions that present pre-fixed answers. For these, all the student needs to do is to select the answers he thinks are the correct ones. These are the *selection-type* questions such as the MCQ, the T/F, and matching items. Then, there are questions that require the student to write one word, a phrase, a sentence, or even a few paragraphs. These are the *supply-type* questions, including FIB, the SA, and essay questions.

The two broad categories of questions have different functions. For some kind of learning, it is sufficient for a student just to be able to pick the correct answer from a few options or choices provided. Or, it is sufficient if he is able to judge correctly whether a statement is true, or to match correctly words in one list with those in another. For other kinds of learning, the student needs to be able to write correctly the expected answers from his memory to show that he knows, remembers, and understands.

Now, let's take a closer look at these various types of questions.

MCQ

This is the most commonly used format. Here is a typical MCQ:

Singapore became an independent nation in the year _____.

   (1) 1945
   (2) 1965
   (3) 1975
   (4) 1985   (   )

As you can see, this MCQ consists of an *item-stem* "*Singapore…year*" and four *options* (choices) "*(1) 1948…(4) 1985*". Among the four options, there is a correct answer (*key*) and three *distracters* (plausible but wrong answers). It is possible that the incomplete sentence "*Singapore…year*" is not used and in its place a question "*In which year did Singapore become an independent nation?*" There is no rule to say which format is better but it is recommended that questions rather than incomplete sentences be used. Here, all a student has to do is to choose the correct answer and write its code (2) in the brackets.

If a computerized answer sheet is used, students need to shade the bubble that has the correct code. Using computerized answer sheet makes it possible to score a very large number of answer scripts within a short time, and also avoid human errors in reading the answers, and entering the marks onto the mark sheet. This is one good reason why MCQs are used so extensively in large-scale nation-level exams. However, its usefulness to small-scale school-based assessment is doubtful, although this has become a common practice.

Another related but more important advantage of using MCQ is that a large number of questions can be included in a test since writing is minimal and time is fully used for reading and selecting to show understanding. This ensures that there is a sufficient coverage of the topics the student is assessed on. From the measurement perspective, broad coverage enhances the content validity (we will talk about *validity* in a later chapter). Moreover, provided that the MCQ items are of a good quality (i.e., having adequate F's and D's), the more questions there are in an exam, the higher the score reliability (we will also talk about *reliability* in a later chapter). In short, by using many MCQs, the students will be more fairly assessed and the test will be fairer.

Some people criticize MCQs for the possibility of guessing correctly when a student does not know the correct answer. This is to some extent true. Since there are usually four options to a MCQ, the student could pick one without thinking and that may turn up to be the correct answer, and the chance is 25% (one in four). This is why some people call it *tikam-tikam* (a kind of traditional roulette). The chance is there but the student may not be always so lucky as to hit the right one all the time.

Thus, logically, increasing the number of options will reduce the chance of correct guessing. So, to minimize correct guessing, instead of having four options, why not make it six options? In fact, research showed that three, four, or five options made very little difference although the convention is to have four options. Teachers using MCQ usually make sure that the correct answers have more or less an equal chance of being coded as (a), (b), (c), or (d). This further reduces chance correctness. Also, good MCQs have options that are carefully worded so that the correct answers are not given away by some cues (for instance, the article *a* excluding options that have a vowel as the first letter thus increasing chance correctness). [3]

Other people criticize MCQ for assessing only the ability to remember facts. It is fashionable for parents to talk about high-order thinking and therefore find fault with MCQ. In fact, MCQs are a very versatile question type. They can assess at almost any level of thinking. Many IQ tests and highly challenging tests such as the SAT (*Scholastic Assessment Test*) and GRE (*Graduate Record Exam*) use MCQ to assess the ability in interpretation and evaluation of information. Look at the MCQ below. Does it assess recall, understanding, or application?

Why does an aquarium need lighting?

    (1) We need light to see the fish.
    (2) Fish need light to see the food.
    (3) To prevent too much carbon dioxide from the plants.
    (4) To prevent plants from growing too fast.

It depends. Had the teacher use the exact words during the lesson, this item assesses recall; a student just needs to remember what the teacher said in the lesson. It assesses understanding if the student relates photosynthesis with plants getting light. If the teacher used an example of photosynthesis without using an aquarium to illustrate, this question assesses application. The differences among the three situations are subtle and require careful thinking.

What has happened during the lesson is not known to school leaders and other teachers. Therefore, it is not possible for them to tell what an MCQ like this assesses without knowing what *the* teacher did in class. This underlines the importance of considering exam together with instruction and not separating one from the other.

Another criticism against MCQ is that it does not assess the ability to organize and present information, that is, integrating and written expression. This criticism is valid but unreasonable. It is like condemning a screwdriver for not being heavy enough to hit a nail, a job better done by a hammer! To be fair, MCQ is *not* meant to assess those abilities in the first place. To do that, it is more proper to use essay-type questions. Besides, nobody says that an exam should use exclusively MCQ. MCQ are but one tool in a toolbox and the user ought to choose wisely.

Yet another criticism is that MCQs may be ambiguous. Take this example:

Which one of the four fruits is different from the others?

    (1)   Durian
    (2)   Orange
    (3)   Apple
    (4)   Grape

The teacher may have in mind that *durian* is a tropical fruit while the others are not. But, a student may choose *orange* because it is juicy (and be marked wrong). His classmate may choose *apple* because it is said to be able to keep the doctor away (where too much of durian may send you to the doctor). Yet another in his class may choose *grape* because only grapes come in bunches. The problem here is not that MCQ is no good but the teacher did not give a clear context to evaluate the options. Things will be different had she phrased the question thus, "Which of these is a tropical fruit?" So, it is obvious that ambiguity is not an inherent weakness of MCQ as a question type. The ambiguity is due to the incompetence (or lack of training) of the setter.

True-false

True-false questions take the form of a statement asking for confirmation or refutation. The same content can be set as a MCQ or a true-false question. For instance, the Independence question can take the form of a true-false item, thus:

| T | F | Singapore became an independent nation in the year 1976. |

One important advantage of using many true-false questions is, like using MCQ, broad coverage that enhances content validity and score reliability. Here, the *tikam-tikam* effect is even greater than MCQ. Fifty percent instead of 25%. In fact, a true-false question can be deemed a two-choice MCQ. The other criticisms and justifications for MCQ may be equally applicable here.

In fact, if students do not have the relevant knowledge and understanding, guessing correctly is not likely, especially if they are told that wrong answers will be penalized, hence the so-called correction formula that adjusts marks for wrong answers. This assumes that all wrong answers are due to blind guessing. In fact, children may have partial knowledge and do not blind-guess. As a matter of fact, in adult life, we always have only partial knowledge of the problems we face and we have to guess as best as we can in trying to solve them. If this is the case, it is good education to train children to guess with partial answers, as a life skill!

Can a true-false question assess higher-order thinking? Yes, for instance assessing children's ability to differentiate between facts and opinions — a critical thinking skill.

Read each statement below carefully and tell whether it is a fact (F) or an opinion (O).

F   O   All normal male Singapore citizens reaching the age of 18 go for National Service.

F   O   All countries must have National Service like what Singapore has.

It is true that true-false questions are seldom used in Singapore schools, perhaps, even as exercises. The marks a student gets from true-false exercises may not be counted to his exam marks, since they are used for practice only. There could be more use of true-false items in assessment for the same reasons as those for MCQ.

Matching

Try this:

Some foods are the main source of nutrients we need. Match them by writing the correct alphabet in the space.

Food	Nutrients
— Egg	a. Carbohydrate
— Fruits	b. Fat
— Nuts	c. Fibre
— Rice	d. Protein
— Vegetable	e. Salt
	f. Vitamins

Matching questions are in fact a multiplicity of multiple-choice questions. The options become less and less in number as you answer the questions. For this reason, the number of options (right column) is always larger than the number of stimulus words (left column) so that even for the last question you still have to think (guess?).

Like MCQ, matching questions have a wide coverage to enhance content validity and score reliability. However, since the stimulus words and options are to be used more than once, they have to be homogeneous, that is, dealing with the same kind of subject matter, for example associating food with the main sources of nutrients as in the question above.

A set of matching questions need not use only single words. They can be more complex than this and can be used in most subjects taught in school. Possible pairings include the following:

Persons and their achievements (Science, Literature, Music, History)
Dates and historical events (History)
Terms and definitions (Science, Math, Geography)
Symbols and concepts (Geography, Math, Science)
Titles and authors (Literature, Arts, Music)

Matching questions are only occasionally used in Singapore schools in spite of the advantages and more use could be made of this versatile question type.

As you have seen, there are many types of objective item formats. They all ask a student to identify the correct answers among the given plausible ones. The large number of questions that can be asked in an exam makes it a fair one in that its content coverage is wide and the scores it yields are reliable. Unfortunately, poorly crafted items give it a bad name.

5. Answers Students Have to Write

As a student moves up the levels, he will have to be able to write his answers. The most commonly used questions for this include fill-in-the-blank, short-answer, and essay-type questions. Let's take a close look at each of these.

Fill-in-the-blank

As the name implies, fill-in-the-blank (FIB) questions ask the student to supply a word or a phrase to complete a sentence that has a word or phrase missing. For example:

Singapore became an independent nation in the year _____ .

Comparing this with the MCQ and true-false questions in the previous chapter, you realize that different types of questions can be set on the same subject matter.

Of course, different types of questions assess different abilities. For the same content, the MCQ question assesses the ability to *identify* the correct answer, the true-false question the ability to *judge* the correctness of the statement, and this FIB question requires the student to *supply* (write) the answer. Although all three questions involve recall, they are somewhat different in terms of the cognitive processes each is engaged with.

The FIB question above looks straightforward. But, is it? What is the correct or acceptable answer? The teacher expects "1965". What if the student writes one of the following?

1. '65.
2. Nineteen-sixty-five.
3. Singapore left Malaysia.
4. Singapore was asked to leave Malaysia.
5. Singapore gained sovereignty.
6. Mr. Lee Kuan Yew became the Prime Minister of Singapore.
7. Mr. Lee Kuan Yew became the first PM of Singapore.
8. Before British Defence Secretary Mr. D. Healy told Mr. Lee Kuan Yew that the British would withdraw from Singapore.

Perhaps, most teachers will accept answers 1 and 2 above as the alternative to *1965*. What about the rest? In fact, children who gave the other answers know more (and in some cases much more) about the Independence. Will they be given the full mark assigned to this seemingly simple question? Or, should they be given even extra marks for knowing more? What if the teacher insists that the only acceptable answer is what appears exactly in the text, *Singapore became an independent nation in the year 1965*?

There was a true story that a Primary One boy filled in the word *reading* for a FIB *"The boy is (   )."* Surprising to the parent, he was marked wrong! When the puzzled parent asked for an explanation, the teacher explained that the question was based on the sentence in the textbook, *The boy is playing*. Here, the teacher set the question intending to assess the student's ability in exactly remembering the text (not a very educational objective, though) but the boy took it as a question assessing his language proficiency. Remember, earlier, we talked about the difference between an attainment test and a proficiency test. The point is relevant here.

However, in language tests, FIB questions are useful for assessing children's ability to supply words and phrases that make grammatical sense. In other subjects, FIB questions are good for assessing children's knowledge of key terms of the subjects. Compare the three FIB questions below and see what they assess.

1. The process by which plants produce their own food is called (<u>photosynthesis</u>).
2. The process by which plants (<u>produce</u>) their own food is called photosynthesis.
3. The process by which plants produce their own food (<u>is</u>) called photosynthesis.

You will agree that the first question is a Science question, the second could be a Science or Language question, and the third definitely a Language question. Thus, the function of the question changes when different words are asked for.

As a general rule, FIB questions for subjects other than Language should focus on specific content words (such as special terms of a subject) and also keep the language of the questions one or more level lower. Thus, preferably, a Science exam for Primary Four should have a language level of Primary Three so that it will not become a Language exam at the same time. This has to do with *validity* which we will talk about later. In short, a good exam should assess what it is supposed to assess and, if possible at all, nothing else.

There is a special kind of FIB called the *cloze passage, cloze procedure* or, simply, *cloze test*. Notice the word *cloze*. In its original sense, *cloze* means *closure*. A typical cloze test looks like the one here. Try it.

The bell has rung and the (   ) was over for the day. The (   ) was very dark and it was (   ) heavily outside. Betsy did not bring (   ) umbrella and so she wondered how (   ) could go home. She used her (   ) phone to call her mother but (   ) one at home picked up the (   ). As the time passed by, more (   ) more of her classmates were gone (   ) she was one of the few (   ) waiting for the rain to stop.

This cloze test is based on the passage below:

The bell has rung and the school was over for the day. The sky was very dark and it was raining heavily outside. Betsy did not bring an umbrella and so she wondered how she could go home. She used her handphone to call her mother but no one at home picked up the phone. As the time passed by, more and more of her classmates were gone and she was one of the few still waiting for the rain to stop.

As you can see, every seventh word of the passage is replaced by a blank. All blanks are of equal length, irrespective of the lengths of the deleted words. This is to avoid giving hints. Moreover, most of the words deleted are content words (e.g., *school, sky, raining*) and a few are function words (e.g., *and, still*).

In the 1950s, an American journalist needed to check the readability of news items he wrote. He argued that if his readers could supply the missing words in a passage, then the passage was meaningful to them. At about the same time, an American psycholinguist theorized that *"Reading is a psycholinguistic guessing game."* This means that when we read, we get the meanings of unfamiliar words by guessing, through the cues provided by words that come before and after the unknown words. We do this often, don't we?

Since then, cloze tests have become rather popular with language teachers and there are modifications to the original idea for some practical reasons. For instance, to make the test easier, cues are given by including the first letter of the omitted words, thus

> The bell has rung and the s(   ) was over for the day. The s(   ) was very dark and it was r(   ) heavily outside. Betsy did not bring a(   ) umbrella and so she wondered how s(   ) could go home....

Instead of omitting words at a regular interval, some teachers omit words of teaching interest, such as pronouns. For instance, if the teacher wants to find out whether her children have mastered the use of pronouns, she may come up with the test below:

> The bell has rung and the school was over for the day. The sky was very dark and (   ) was raining heavily outside. Betsy did not bring an umbrella and so (   ) wondered how (   ) could go home. (   ) used (   ) hand phone to call (   ) mother but no one at home picked up the phone. As the time passed by, more and more of (   ) classmates were gone and (   ) was one of the few still waiting for the rain to stop.

The teacher may call this a *pronoun cloze test,* but I will just call it a *pronoun test* because, strictly speaking, it is not a cloze test as such. The reason is simple and statistical. When words are deleted at a regular interval (say, every seventh word), the deletions form a *systematic sample* of the language and will cover a variety of words (common names, adjectives, verbs, adverbs, articles, etc., etc.) that are typical of the language. When only certain kind of words (e.g., pronouns) are omitted, the deletions are not random and thus violates the basic theoretical assumption of the cloze test.

There are a few acceptable answers all making sense, some better than the others. Likewise, a cloze test can be marked in two ways, the Exact Word Method and the Acceptable Word Method.

As the name implies, when the Exact Word Method is used, only words that are exactly the same in the original text are accepted. Other words are not given marks even if they make sense. On the other hand, the Acceptable Word Method accepts any words that make sense close enough to the original meanings.

As can be expected, the Exact Word Method will give a student a lower mark than does the Acceptable Word Method. Research has shown that the two methods rank children very much the same way. That is to say, if a student scores high when the Exact Word Method is used, he is very likely to score high also when the Acceptable Word Method is used. [4]

However, to teachers, the two methods have different implications. The Exact Word Method is easier to use and less time-consuming to mark. All they need to do is to follow religiously the scoring key looking for exact words. In spite of this convenience, some teachers object to the inflexibility of this method, seeing it as penalizing children who seem to have a better command of language and not giving children a chance. Moreover, it emphasizes route learning that is un-educational.

When using the Acceptable Word Method, the teachers need to assess the acceptability every time a word that is not the original one comes up. And, for this, they need to compile a list of acceptable words for reference to ensure all teachers marking the same paper use the same standard so as to be fair to all students. Without such a list, different teachers may accept or reject words that are meaningful in the context of the passage and this lower inter-rater agreement and affects score reliability.

Short-answer questions

A short-answer question is in fact a FIB question asking a student to supply his own answer. Here he has to write more words, usually a phrase, to complete an incomplete sentence or just answer a simple question. Look at this example:

> Photosynthesis is the process by which (*plants make food*).

Another teacher may set the question like this:

> Photosynthesis is (*the process by which plants make food*).

Both questions are OK, except that the second asks for more and perhaps unnecessary writing. In this case, the second question assesses a mixture of Science knowledge as well as English Language. Of course, the teacher may justify by saying that she intends to assess the knowledge that photosynthesis is a process and not a product. In fact, there are teachers who believe that every lesson is a language lesson and therefore every exam must also assess language ability at the same time. This sounds reasonable, but assessing Science and English Language at the same time reduces the validity of the exams. Thus, when a student scores high, we do not know whether he is good in subject knowledge or language, and *vice versa*.

Sometimes, a short-answer question may be set in such a way that several answers are more or less equally acceptable. For example:

> Carnivorous animals are (   ).

Children may give the following answers that are all acceptable:

> *tiger, lion, wolf, and cat.*
> *tigers, wolves, cats, and lions.*
> *animals that eat other animals for food.*
> *animals that prey on other animals.*
> *meat-eating animals.*
> *meat-eaters.*

Thus, unless teachers who mark the same question have first compiled a comprehensive list of acceptable answers, some children are likely to be penalized because of lack of inter-rater agreement. Had the teacher set the question as shown below, then only the first two answers are acceptable.

Four examples of carnivorous animals are (   ), (   ), (   ), and (   ).

Had the teacher set the following question, then the last two answers can be accepted.

Animals grouped as carnivorous animals are (   ).

Had the teacher set the question below, then only the third and fourth answers are acceptable.

To feed themselves, carnivorous animals are animals that (   ).

Thus, a good short-answer question ought to provide a specific context so that students know clearly what they are supposed to write, and how much to write. For instance, the question *"Examples of carnivorous animals are...."* If a student knows a large number of such animals, should he write all their names to answer this question? If the blank is long, should he continue to the end of it and then stops. Or, should he continue on the next page to write all the names he knows? Of course, the question *"Four examples of carnivorous animals are _____"* is specific. Here, the teacher can safely assume that if a student is able to name four such animals, he knows what carnivorous animals are.

Essay-type questions

As a student moves up the class level, he will face more questions that are more complex. These are the essay-type questions (not necessarily writing an essay as such). The simplest essay questions ask for simple answers. For instance,

| In which year did Singapore become an independent nation? |
| What is photosynthesis? |
| What are carnivorous animals? |

These simply ask questions instead of presenting incomplete sentences. The answers listed earlier for these questions are acceptable. But there may be additional problems. For instance, to the question on photosynthesis, a student writes, *"Photo mean light. Synthesis means putting together."* Is this acceptable? Another student's answer is, *"Photo mean light. Synthesis means putting together. The green substance of leaves called chlorophyll uses carbon dioxide, water, and sunlight to produce food."* Should he get more than the full mark for this question?

For another example, a student writes his answer to the question on carnivorous animals, thus, *"Carnivorous animals are animals that eat other animals for food."* Another writes only *"Animals that eat other animals for food"* or just *"animals that eat other animals."* Another student gives the definition with examples and yet another gives only examples without the definition. Are all these acceptable? This is where all great minds (of teachers) do not think alike! And, will the student lose a mark or two for not writing a capitalised *A*?

When teachers do not agree on the acceptable answers, the trustworthiness of score becomes suspect. More importantly, lack of consistency in marking makes the exams unfair. Of course, some teachers were trained in setting exams and they take care to ensure the quality of the papers they design and ensure consistency in marking. Some other teachers were not trained to set exams and they learned on the job and gained experience as well.

Normally, an essay-type question asks for much more than such a short answer. Below is an actual question from a large-scale exam years back.

Name four vitamins and give a detailed account of the sources and functions of each. In each case, say if they can be stored in the body, and whether they are affected by heat.

This question has the following components that make an answer:

1. Name of vitamin
2. Sources
3. Functions
4. Retention in the body
5. Effect of heat

And, don't forget that each of these is to be multiplied by four! While many of these components have specific answers, there is another difficulty with *detailed account*. What is detailed enough for one teacher may be skimpy to another, and the marks for the same answer given by the two teachers will be different.

Besides, teachers have different ideas of what is good language expressions and handwriting. The ability levels of the children they have been teaching for years also influence their expectations. In fact, in an experiment (more about this later), teachers who gave lower marks are from the so-called *better* schools and vice versa. This is perfectly understandable. Teachers in the first group have seen much better answers and therefore set higher expectation and hence gave lower marks, and vice versa.

The question to ask here is, if such inconsistency can happen with a question that is scientific and factual in nature (and hence can be more objectively marked), what will happen to the less scientific subjects? Perhaps, essay-type question is not suitable for subject matter like this, and other forms of questions should have been considered and used.

The use of marking schemes (rubrics) and model answers may help, but up to a point only. And, sometimes, these devices may make the problem worse by magnifying marker idiosyncrasy. For instance, it is not impossible that a strict marker marks strictly several times, since the marking scheme has several components. Thus, his strictness is not only present but repeated.

There is another hidden problem of essay-type questions. In an exam where such questions are used, the tradition is that choices of questions are allowed, such as "*Answer any two of the five questions.*" The reasons for this are not known — just like any other long-lived tradition, for instance setting a passing mark at 50%. The one reason often cited is "to give children a chance." What then is the problem?

To understand the problem, imagine there are five bathroom scales in front of you. They all look alike. You are to choose any two of the five to take your weight. So, there are actually 10 different pairs you can choose from. Without your knowledge, some of the five scales are 'difficult' ones because they have harder springs, other are 'easy' for they have softer springs. Now, you know what will happen to your body weight (not your body, of course). If you happen to choose two with harder springs, your weight is underestimated. On the other hand, you may get a weight heavier than you actually are if you have chosen two with softer springs. Do you trust the weights you get from different combinations of the five scales? Remember, your actual weight is a constant and does not change irrespective of which scales you have chosen.

The same problem is for *Answer any two of the five questions.* Questions are of different levels of difficulties. When different children have the freedom to choose any combination of two, it appears fair since they have equal chance in choosing the questions. But, in fact, they are assessed with different yardsticks made up of different combinations of two questions. So, in this section of the exam, there are in fact 10 pairs of topics. Imagine the students are measured for their heights using 10 different yardsticks, some longer and some shorter!

True, it is a tradition and tradition dies hard. Children (and their parents) may object to no choices being given to essay-type questions, but they need be aware of the pitfall that this is in fact not fair to the children. Of course, if the teacher is able to make all questions more or less equal in difficulty, the problem will not arise. But, this is easier said than done because the actual facilities (Fs) can be known only after but not before the exam is taken.

Incidentally, have you ever taken an exam in which you were asked to answer any five of the 10 questions? Do you know how many combinations there were? As many as 252! If all combinations are to be printed separately for you to choose, the exam paper will run into a book! So, by asking you to choose any five of 10 questions, paper (and trees) is saved.

Another problem of essay-type questions is when they are used in English Language exams where children are asked to write essays. An essay has two aspects, its content (or substance or what it is about) and expression (the use of language or how it presents the substance). Normally, a marking scheme for assessing essays will spell out how many marks are to be given to the several components such as content, vocabulary, grammar, punctuation, organisation, etc.

While vocabulary, grammar, punctuation, and organisation are more clear-cut (these being writing skills), content may pose a problem of fairness. Compare these two essay titles given to students for writing essays: *An hour on the Singapore Flyer* and *An hour on the Moon*. They look similar, don't they? Yes, they look alike.

Children who for some reasons have not been to the Flyer will have very little to write and will not be able to write substance-rich essays that get more marks for content. On the other hand, no children have been to the Moon (not yet). So, all of them have little to write about. What they write will be mostly imaginative. Thus, the first title is not a fair one. If some children have not been there because of the financial condition of the family, then the essays they write reflects their poorer home condition, and the essay question becomes a proxy measure of socio-economic status of their families and not so much their ability to express themselves in writing. Of course, children from such homes also tend to be weaker in language as many research studies have shown, but this is not the point of concern here. [5]

On the other hand, the title on a trip to the moon will be much fairer to all children, since all will have no relevant experience to write about. No doubt, a few children may have read books about the moon and therefore have some advantages over those who have not, on the whole, the goodness of the essays written depends very much on the children's imagination. Such creative ability of imagination is the essence of great literature.

Up till now, we have looked at various types of questions that are commonly used for assessment. They have specific functions, strengths, and weaknesses. This means no question type is perfect and over-reliance on or exclusive use of any of them will make an exam yield scores less reliable and valid than it should be, that is, less fair.

Thus, for a student to have fair exams, we need to rely on his teachers' judicious choice of question types, question designing, and consistent marking. All these, in turn, depend on proper teacher training in exam skills.

6. T-score: What Is It, and Why?

When a student is in Primary 6, he will have to sit for the Primary School Leaving Exam (PSLE) sometime in October. In the PSLE, there are four exam papers — English Language, Mother Tongue Language, Mathematics, and Science.

When the exam is over, the marks for these four subjects are reported in terms of T-scores. The total of the T-scores, called T-Aggregate, is then used for assigning the student to one of the school choices made on his behalf by his parent. As we all know, different secondary schools take in children with different T-Aggregates. We also know that children who have gotten higher T-Aggregates go to the 'better' Streams and schools.

Typically, the 'better' schools cream off children who have T-Aggregates greater than 200 or even higher. The reason (and its assumption) is that such children are more academically inclined and capable of benefiting from further schooling at the secondary level. Children not going to such schools are assigned to other secondary schools of lesser academic reputation. As far as the correlation (relationship) between PSLE and the GCE 'O'-Level Exam is concerned, this is a reasonable assumption because children who have done better in the PSLE tend also to do better in the 'O'-Level Exam four years later.

However, this apparently rational approach to student movement has over the years unheedingly created a tension among some parents, especially those whose children missed the opportunity to get into their coveted 'prime' secondary schools by small margins of a few points in the T-Aggregate. Besides, it is an oft-voiced criticism that exclusive

43

focusing on academic achievement is undesirable and assessment of students needs to also consider their other strengths and non-academic talent.

It is for such reasons that the Singapore Ministry of Education announced that the T-Aggregates will be replaced by Achievement Levels which groups (raw) scores for the four subjects into eight groups which, as announced, will also better reflect a student's level of achievement by grading each student on his individual performance regardless of how the cohort performance (https://www.gov.sg/news/content/no-more-psle-t-scores-from-2021). However, this scheme will be implemented only in 2021 while there will be continuous, rigorous, and thorough testing of the new scoring and posting systems. This is what is promised and the actual effects and effectiveness will be known only a few years later. In the meantime, the current system will continue.

It is necessary to point out here that *T-score* and *T-Aggregate* are two different, though somewhat related, concepts: T-score is the result of T-transformation (standardization) to offset the different means and standard deviations to ensure comparability of scores for different subjects. This is to prevent scores from a broader distribution to have undue advantage over those from narrower distributions. (This concept will be made clear with an analogy of different currencies later.) On the other hand, T-Aggregate is the result of a simple operation of adding up T-scores for a total, weighted or otherwise. Note that *standardization* (to get T-score) and *summation* (to get T-Aggregate) are conceptually unrelated and they serve different functions. In short, standardization is to ensure data quality and summation is to facilitate data utilization and the two concepts and functions need to be kept distinct.

Same marks, different meanings

What in fact is a T-score and why does PSLE report results using T-scores? For this, we have to use the body weight analogy once more.

Imagine you have four bathroom scales (representing the four examined subjects, of course) that look rather different from one another. You step on all four of them in turn and you always get 62 kg. So, you think the scales are OK. What you do not know is that each has a spring that is harder or weaker than the rest. But, since 62 = 62 = 62 = 62, you think the scales measure your weight in the same way and anyone of the 62 is as good as any other one. Right? Wrong!

The four PSLE papers are not of the same length; they do not have the same number of questions and hence do not have the same maximum total marks. Even if they have the same number of questions, the results of the children on each of the four exam papers are not the same. One paper may have a higher *average* (*mean*) than the others. Also, one paper may spread out the children much wider than the others, such that the difference between the highest and the lowest marks (statistically called *range*) of one paper is much greater (or smaller) than that of the others. Technically, the lowest-to-highest spread of scores is calculated in terms of a statistic called the *standard deviation* (SD).

This is getting a bit technical. But let us try to understand this important aspect of exam (any exam, not necessarily the PSLE) marks. We will look at a hypothetical but realistic case. Which of the two children whose scores for a school-based exam shown below is a 'better' one?

Subject	Albert	Alfred
English Language	76	68
Mother Tongue Language	83	76
Mathematics	78	83
Science	68	78
Total	305	305

More likely than not, you will say Albert is as good as Alfred. That's commonsense. Here, you take, for example, Albert's 76 for English Language as equal to Alfred's 76 for Mother Tongue Language. Also, Albert's 83 for Mother Tongue is taken to be equal to Alfred's 83 for Math, and so on. After all, they both get a total mark of 305. Therefore, Albert and Alfred are equally good academically, because they have the same total *raw marks*. What's wrong with this?

To show what is wrong with this, let's look at the table below with the same number but different 'subjects' (currencies). This time, we talk about money; talking about money makes things easier and clearer!

Currency	Albert's uncle	Alfred's uncle
Singapore Dollar	76	68
US Dollar	83	76
Japanese Yen	78	83
Chinese Yuan	68	78
Total	305	305

Do you think the two uncles have the same amount of cash in their pockets? You won't, definitely, because you know too well that 76 SGD can buy you many cans of Coca Cola while 76 yen can't buy you even one can. In short, different currencies have different buying power (Purchasing Power Parity or PPP, to make it more important-sounding). We can do some simple calculation and convert all monies to USD as shown in the table below.

Currency	USD equivalent as of 6 March 2016	Albert's uncle	Alfred's uncle
Singapore Dollar	0.730	55.48	49.64
US Dollar	1.000	83.00	76.00
Japanese Yen	0.009	0.69	0.73
China's Yuan	0.150	10.20	11.70
Total	—	149.37	138.07

Now it is clear that, if this money is all that the uncles have, Albert's is richer than Alfred's. But, what has buying power and exchange rates got to do with PSLE results?

As you know, the four PSLE papers have different lengths in terms of the numbers of questions in each of them. Even if the papers have the same number of questions (lengths), the average performance (means) are different for different subjects. The lowest and the highest marks for English Language may be 75 and 115, with a mean (average) of 85 and the scores spread the children over a range of 40 (giving a SD around, say, 6). At the same time, the lowest mark for Science may be 25 and highest 55, with a mean of, say, 35 and the scores spread over a range of 30 (giving a standard deviation of around, say, 4).

Obviously, these two subjects do not have the same 'buying power'. You may think that English Language is an easier paper (since the average is 85) than Science (having a mean of on 35). This may and may not be correct for three reasons. First, the higher mean for English Language may be due to it having much more questions. Secondly, there is no way we can say that one mark for English is equivalent to one mark for Science. That is, we cannot be sure that getting one mark for English Language requires the same mental ability and effort to get one mark for Science. Thirdly (and, this is the most critical but more often than not unheeded), the statistical fact is that a score from a distribution with a greater spread (indicated by a greater range or SD) is automatically weighted more when the raw scores from several tests are simply added to derive the total score. This makes scores for distributions with smaller spreads less powerful in the total raw scores, thus rendering these tests less effective than intended.

Now, the meaninglessness of equating Albert with Alfred simply because both get 305 as the total marks is clear. The next question is, what can we do?

Before we go back to Albert's and Alfred's exam results, let us solve the uncles' currency problem first. What are you to do with the different currencies? Of course, you use the exchange rates to convert them all to the same 'dollar'. But, there are four of them, which one do we use? Isn't it more convenient to convert all currencies into just only one currency? OK, let's take USD since it has been used as the International Dollar for cross-nation conversion. Once we convert the monies into US dollars, we can compare them correctly. We should do something similar with the exam results.

Here, we convert all marks to the T-score as used for reporting PSLE results. The T-score is a score-conversion technique that sets arbitrarily the mean at 50 (to represent the average ability in whichever subject). The T-scale also has an arbitrary standard deviation of 10. With this conversion, all marks will be transformed into marks falling with the range of zero to 100, theoretically. In reality, the lowest T-score is around 20 and the highest around 80, giving a spread of 60 that is more than sufficient for sorting children. This is the process of *standardization* and the T-scores are *standard scores*. Without standardization, raw scores for one subject are apples and those for another subject are oranges.

Some simple stats

But, to use the T-scale, we need to know for each subject its mean and SD. As you recall, the *mean* is what we usually call the *average* that is a *representative* or the *typical performance* of the children who have taken the test. You also recall that the SD shows how widely spreading out the children are away from the mean. With these two bits of information, we are ready to convert raw marks (those given by the marker according to the marking scheme) into T-score (a form of standard score). The formula is:

$$\text{T - score} = \frac{\text{A student's raw mark} - \text{Mean of raw marks of all children}}{\text{Standard deviation of raw marks}} \times 10 + 50$$

For example, if English Language has a mean of 60 and a standard deviation of 8, then Albert's 76 for English Language is equivalent to a T-score of 70, and Alfred's 68 becomes T = 60. How do these come about?

In Albert's case,

$$\text{T - score} = \frac{76 - 60}{8} \times 10 + 50 = \frac{16}{8} \times 10 + 50 = 2 \times 10 + 50 = 70$$

And, in Alfred's case,

$$\text{T - score} = \frac{68 - 60}{8} \times 10 + 50 = \frac{8}{8} \times 10 + 50 = 1 \times 10 + 50 = 60$$

Have we shortchanged them, since their marks seem to have shrunk from 76 to 70 for Albert and 68 to 60 for Alfred? No, they still keep their relative merits, but the difference between them has been converted (standardized) to the same SD unit. This is just like converting SGD to USD; although they may look poorer in US dollars but their relative buying power remains unaffected. Now, let us do the same for all their marks. The results are shown in the table below:

Subject	Mean	Standard deviation	Albert		Alfred	
			Mark	T-score	Mark	T-score
English Language	60	8	76	70	68	60
Mother Tongue	75	4	83	70	76	53
Mathematics	55	15	78	65	83	69
Science	60	10	68	58	78	68
Total	—	—	305	263	305	249

Now the picture is clear. Albert has T-Aggregate of 263 and Alfred a T-Aggregate of 249: Albert did better than Alfred in the PSLE, in spite of the equal raw totals.

Equals are not equivalents

The importance and usefulness of T-scores can be seen from the two examples below.

As you can see from the table above, Alfred got 68 for English Language and 76 for Mother Tongue Language. Is he better in Mother Tongue Language than he is in English language? Why do you say so? Yes, Alfred is better in Mother Tongue Language than in English Language; because 76 is greater than 68, therefore he is better in Mother Tongue. Again, wrong!

If you look at Alfred's T-scores for the two subjects, the T-score for English Language is 60 but that for Mother Tongue Language 53. Thus, in spite of the lower raw mark for English Language, he is better in English Language than in Mother Tongue language. How can a lower raw score indicate a better performance? You disagree.

The reason is this. Alfred is one student among many others (say, 100 for the same level in the same school) who have taken the same tests. Imagine that the teacher asks the children to line up in ascending order of their English Language marks. Given the mean and the SD calculated from the raw marks for this subject, and given that he has a T-score of 60, Alfred stands at a point where there are 83 children behind him. That is to say, he is at the 84th percentile, technically speaking. Likewise, given the mean and the SD for the Mother Tongue Language, and given that he has a T-score of 53 for this subject, he stands at a point where 52 children are behind him. He has a 53rd percentile for Mother Tongue Language. (If you wonder how the numbers of children behind Alfred come about, please wait until we talk about the Normal Curve, soon. For the time being just trust me.)

Since Alfred stands far ahead of his peers in English Language than he does for Mother Tongue Language, he must be better in English Language than in Mother Tongue Language, although he obtained higher raw marks for the latter. Surely you have noticed by now that we are comparing Alfred's performance in the two subjects by comparing *how much better he is than his peers are in the same two subjects.*

When we compare and interpret the performance of one student with reference to the performance of all other children who have taken the same test, we are using what is technically called *norm-referencing*. The concern here is "who is better", not "what can he do". In the main, this is the way we use to group children in our education system.

Take another example. Albert got 76 for English Language and 83 for Mother Tongue Language. Is he better in English Language than in Mother Tongue Language? This time you will say "No", because when you look at his T-scores for the two subjects, they are both 70. So, you conclude that Albert is equally good in the two Languages. Correct! If we ask Albert and his peers to line up according to their marks for the two subjects, on both occasions, Albert will be far ahead of his peers, having a 98th percentile for both subjects.

The normal curve

You may skip this section if you wish, but I urge you to read on, *for your own good*, as we always say.

The conversion of raw marks to T-scores illustrated above (and as done for the PSLE) has one important assumption, that is, the marks are *normally distributed*. What's that?

In large-scale national exams, the number of children taking the same papers is very large. Each year, there are around 35,000 to 40,000 children taking the PSLE. (But, the number keeps shrinking because we are not reproducing enough, so much so that schools have to be merged. This of course is an important national issue which is beyond the scope of this book.) Even at the school level, at each class level there are around 200 to 240 children. Such a number justifies the assumption of normal distribution, if the tests are set with suitable facilities (F's) for the intended students.

The normally distributed marks will give a bell-shaped curve when plotted. The normal curve (1) is symmetrical, that is, if we fold the curve right at the middle, the left and the right halves will overlap exactly or almost so; (2) has more marks concentrating in the middle, tallest at the centre where the mean is to be found; (3) tapers off when moving away from the middle, having less and less students getting higher/lower marks. It is such characteristics that give us the bell-shape curve. [6, 7] The normal curve is shown below:

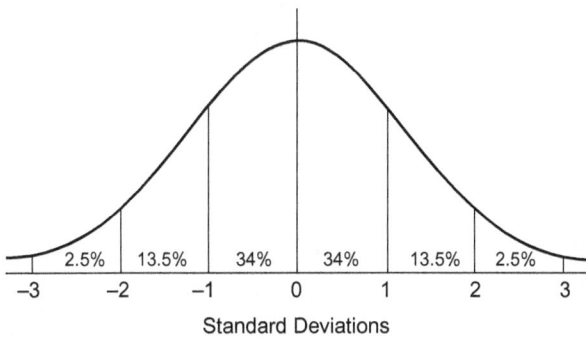

Standard Deviations

Moreover, we can divide the normal curve into many segments, usually six for practical purposes, at one-SD intervals. Theoretically speaking, the one segment encompassed by a line drawn up from the mean, a line drawn up at one-SD higher than the mean, the baseline, and the curve above it, will include around 34% of the children. Over to the other side of the mean (that is, one SD below the mean) will cover another 34%. Thus, the area within the boundaries of one-SD above the mean and one below will include 68% children. These are, by educational and psychological definitions, the *normal* children. (Please do not confuse this *normal* with the so-called *Normal Stream* as Singapore uses the word.)

Then, beyond this middle group of students (or the average or *normal* students) are, of course, the better and, on the other side, the weaker ones. Theoretically speaking again, between the first and the second SDs above the mean, there are another 14% children who are 'above average'. This leaves us with 2% at the top end (the 'best'). Going to the other side, there are 14% much weaker ones and 2% very weak ones.

Many years ago, when Professor F. Warburton of the University of Manchester said in a BBC interview that half of the British population is below average in intelligence, he shocked England like a 6.5 earthquake. But, he was telling the truth, nothing but the truth! Intelligence tests the world over are scaled to have a mean of 100 (and a SD of 15). So, by definition, 50% of the population (British, Singaporean, or any other) will have IQ lower than the mean (average) of 100!

7. What Is a Good Mark?

School leaders and teachers always wish that their students get good marks, especially for national exams. Parents are naturally concerned about the marks their children get from assessment, tests and exams, within and beyond the school campus. All three parties invariably expect good marks. But, then, what is a good mark — good in what sense?

Passing marks

In the old days when I was a secondary school boy in a Chinese school, the passing mark was 60. For my friends who attended the then English schools, the passing mark was 40. When our two language streams came together through integration, the pass mark was changed to 50. Was this a compromise between 40 and 60? Nobody seems to know. The real question is not how these passing marks came about but what does it tell you about the performance in exams.

By now, you would have realized that a mark standing alone has no meaning; to understand or interpret the mark meaningfully, you need relevant information such as (a) how other children who have taken the same test scored, or (b) how many questions have the student answered correctly. In short, you need a frame of reference to understand the student's performance in a meaningful manner, not just the *lonely* mark.

If you have information (a), you can find out how better a student is on the test when compared with his classmates; for instance, he is better than 80% of them, so he stands at the 81st percentile. This is the so-called *norm-referencing* interpretation of the scores.

Or, if you have information (b), you can tell that the student has spelt correctly 32 of the 40 words of a spelling test, and assuming that these words have been chosen to suit the level of children of your student's age, then he got 80% correct. If for some good reasons (say, part research or experience) you considered 75% as the cut-score (criterion), he scored 80% and therefore meets the criterion and passes the test. This is, in a sense, the *criterion-referencing* interpretation of test results.

A passing mark, in fact, represents the expectation with certain assumptions. First, we assume that the test has been set at a level suited to the group of students we assess. Then, we assume that the passing mark is able to separate those who can (the sheep) from those who can't (the goats), with little uncertainty (called *error* in measurement lingo). And, we further assume that we are clear about what the test results will be used for.

To satisfy the first condition, test setters have the past papers to refer to so that a new test is not grossly different from those used in previous years. Otherwise, the passing rate for the new test will be very different from those of the past years, with much more distinctions, passes, or failures. In other words, the passing rate is controlled year over year by maintaining the difficulty levels of tests and the proportion of test-taking children *allowed* to 'pass'. Too obvious deviation from the 'standard' in public exams will puzzle or upset parents and cause alarm to the public.

For the second condition, when all the marks are plotted as a distribution curve, the number of students scoring around the passing mark should be as low as possible to minimize error in passing/failing decision. The reason for this is simple. Let's take the passing mark of 50. If out of 300 children taking the test and 60 of them scored around this passing mark, usually and for administrative convenience, those who scored 50 will get a pass and those who get 49 will fail. However, because test scores are fallible (i.e., far from being perfectly stable), many of those who failed (scoring near 49) by one or even a few marks may actually pass if they were given a second chance to take the same test another time. On the other hand, if the number of children scoring around the passing mark of 50 is small, then only a very small proportion may swap places (from pass to fail and vice versa). This is a question about *score reliability* which we will discuss in the next chapter.

Passing a wrong student is just as costly as failing a wrong one, especially in our context where manpower is scarce and precious. But, then, such measurement error (not *mistake* in the usual sense but fluctuation in the statistical sense) is practically inevitable because of the imperfection of the technology of test setting, not until we are able to set exams which yield scores of perfect reliability. In fact, research on setting cut-scores (or passing marks) has been carried out especially at the Educational Testing Service at Princeton, USA. [8]

As for the third condition, the usual school-based test is for the purpose of gauging the students' performance, it is a general purpose test that will preferably yield an approximation of the normal curve for the marks. However, for special purposes, such as scholarships or special programmes, due to the smaller number of places available and the high cost involved, the error rates should be very low so that the benefits go to the right students and the money is well spent. For such tests, the normal curve does not apply and specially designed tests are necessary.

In sum, a passing mark without due consideration for these conditions will be misleading and will result in more wrong decisions being made. The passing mark is not a magic number. It is a number that should help in making correct decisions.

A good mark

Is 100 a good mark? Yes, it's a perfect mark. No, wrong! If this 100 is for the *Standard Achievement Test* (SAT), a popular American test for selecting university applicants in USA, which has a maximum score of 1600, then, 100 is a very, very poor score, because it lies far below the possible minimum score of 400 of the test!

Why then do many parents (and teachers and school leaders) take 100 as a very good or perfect mark? It is because they are so used to see 100% as the perfect situation in life (and tests), with little thought of what makes a perfect situation. We use 100% metaphorically to signify perfection. This is a misuse of the concept of percentage. Whenever we use percentage, we should be clear about "percent of *what*". For example, when you buy a pair of new glasses and you are very satisfied with it, you may say, "It fits me 100%" when you should say "It fits me perfectly."

If you say, "It's 80% perfect", what do you mean? Does that mean you are not happy with 20% of the glasses, and can you tell which part?

A teacher gives a 50-word spelling test and a boy spells all words correctly. He is awarded a mark of 100, much to his (and his parents') delight. Does this mean he is perfect in spelling? Maybe, and maybe not. If the boy is in Primary Four and the 50 words come from a wordlist for Primary Six, you have really something to celebrate. What if the words all come from a wordlist for Primary Two? All it says is that the Primary Four boy is a perfect Primary Two speller; nothing fantastic. You won't go celebrating, although the 100 gives you a good feeling all the same.

Conversely, if the test consists of words suitable for very high level of education such as those used in the GRE (Graduate Record Exam) and if the boy gets a very low score, there is nothing wrong with his spelling ability and nothing to be sad about it. It should be that way! The only thing you can say is that the teacher has not been fair or she needs basic training in setting exam papers. (We will discuss this in the chapter on above-level testing.)

Improvement?

Albert got 75 for his Mathematics test last month. For this month, he also got 75. His mother was a bit disappointed because she expected him to show improvement after all the expensive coaching his tutor has provided. Alex's mark for the last English test was 70 and this time it was 65, to his mother's horror, as she thought he should show improvement after she spent so much time coaching him. And, Alvin gets 10 marks more for the Mother Tongue Language test this week, compared with the one last month; his mother, of course, was very happy that he did improve as she has paid the private tutor handsomely.

All three mothers were wrong!

Albert did not necessarily maintain status quo. Alex did not necessarily retrogress. And, Alvin did not necessarily improve. It all depends!

When we compare two marks obtained by the same student for two different tests for the same subject, we can easily be misled by the difference between marks or the lack of it. Here again, the oft-repeated concept that marks stand alone has no meaning.

The two Math tests Albert took with one month in between most likely are not the same test. The teacher has no reason to give the same test twice (unless she is doing an action research project). Most likely, the two tests covered different topics and the second test was most likely a more difficult one, since the syllabus normally listed more difficult topics after easier ones. At most, the topics could be equally difficult but involving entirely different mathematical concepts, say, Weight and Area. So, although Albert got 75 for both tests and if the later one was more difficult than the earlier one, Albert in fact has improved in his learning. The problem is that such gain was not reflected in the marks. In short, Albert's second 75 is actually better than his first 75.

By the same token, Alex's five marks less in the second English test may not mean he has lost some of his proficiency in English. It may even be the contrary, if the second test was much more difficult than the first.

Likewise, Alvin might not have improved in spite of the 'better' mark; it could be due to the much lower difficulty level of the second test.

Although we have been talking about individual children, the same principle goes for classes, schools, and the whole system. An increase in passing rate does not necessarily reflect improvement. Conversely, a decrease may not mean losing steam. Of course, the same passing rate for two years need not be interpreted as lack of improvement. The crucial thing here is the relative difficulty levels of the two tests.

Exam results are highly emotionally charged, for students, teachers, school leaders, parents and the system. When a school has an increase in, say, PSLE passes, the teachers, the school leaders, the students (and not forgetting their parents) are naturally happy. When a school has a decrease in passing rate, they are naturally unhappy. But, do not rush into celebration or crying before checking the difficulty levels of the two years' papers. Such checking is not only professionally sound but also essential for correct interpretation of exam results.

These fictitious examples boil down to one fact: a mark standing alone has no meaning and it should be interpreted with reference to some other relevant information which may or may not be available to you. In this sense, a mark is relative, don't take it as absolute. So, what is a good mark? It depends.

8. Can Exams be Trusted?

This seems to be a foregone conclusion; we have been trusting exams a lot, in spite of the occasional doubting. Since the weight watching analogy has served us well up to now, we shall continue to use it to examine the trustworthiness of exams.

Reliability

We have used the word *reliability* several times without explaining what it means. This is the time we get a clear picture of it.

How do you check whether your bathroom scale is trustworthy? You can read for your body weight, step down, step on the scale again and do a second reading, and a third reading, and so on, until you feel confident that you can trust the scale. If the scale is in good shape, the several readings you get should be very close, or exactly the same, or almost so with very small variations. Thus, you take the test of your weight several times and expect to get very similar results. Let's call this kind of consistency *test-retest reliability.*

When a student and his classmates take an exam together, each gets a mark according to the answers they have given. Suppose their teacher, for some reasons, gets the children to take the same exam a second time afterward, with little time gap, say, half an hour later. Now, each student has two marks for the same exam. What do you expect of the two sets of marks? They should be the same, right? Yes, the two marks for each student may not be exactly the same, but they should be very much the same, perhaps, with one or two marks difference.

This should be the case if the exam is made up of objective questions such as MCQ. We can reasonably expect this because the correct answers for MCQ (and other type of objective questions) have been decided upon when the questions were set. This gives the so-called keyed answers. Whoever marks the papers are supposed to follow strictly the keys and returns the same results. Thus, it makes no difference whether the teacher or another teacher or even a helpful clerk marks the papers as long as she follows the keys strictly. Nowadays, teachers may make the computer do the marking by first keying in the keys (or their codes such as *a*, *b*, *c*, and *d*), then key in the children' answers, and let the computer do the checking (marking). In fact, a large part of PSLE papers takes the form of objective questions and these are computer-marked, for fast and accurate marking.

Imagine you have two or more bathroom scales of the same type (an unlikely event). To check whether the scales give you trustworthy information about your body weight, you step on them one after another. What do you expect? You expect the same readings or there about. As the scales are supposed to be equally effective in measuring your weight, the consistency among the readings can be called *equivalent-form reliability*, since the two or more scales are supposed to be highly similar or equivalent.

A teacher follows the same TOS (test blueprint) and sets two papers made up of similar objective questions. She makes sure that each pair of questions for the two sets assess the same knowledge, skills, or under-standing though worded slightly differently. Now she has two equivalent (or parallel) forms of the same exam. If she gets the children to take these two exams in one sitting, the results for the two sets of questions should be very close, giving a small margin of differences since the questions are not exactly the same.

There is a way of using the computer to calculate a statistic called *cor-relation coefficient* to find out exactly how close the two sets of marks are. Such a correlation coefficient will be equal to 1.00 when the two sets of marks are exactly the same, and will be lower than 1.00 when there are some differences between the two sets. If the two sets are totally inconsist-ent with each other, the coefficient will go down nearer to 0.00. In this case, students who get high marks the first time may get a high, mediocre, or low mark the second time. And, in the most unlikely event, when students who get high marks on the first exam always get low marks on the second, and vice versa, the coefficient will be negative.

American research shows that exams designed by teachers usually have moderate score reliability. The reliabilities vary from 0.35 to 0.90, averaging about 0.70. However, for standardized exams, the reliability coefficients ought to be 0.90 or higher before the exams are published for purposes such as making decision on the individual children. [9]

There are other ways of checking score reliability where the weight watching analogy cannot be used in a practical sense, but weighting is still a good analogy. Imagine that you have bought a big basket of 30 durians and you wanted to know the total weight. (Of course, you are more interested in the flavour and taste of the durians than their weight.) You divided them into two lots: the first half at the top of the basket and the second half at the bottom. You weighted the two lots separately and found the weights to be about equal. So, the weight of the full basket seemed to be consistent; this is analogous to the *split-half reliability*. This has to be upgraded to the full-length reliability by the *Spearman-Brown Prophecy Formula*, since the reliability is for only half of the test.

However, that is only one of so many ways of dividing the durians into two halves. How do you know that is the best way of dividing? So, you take the first durian and pair it with another one and recorded their respective weights. When you have finished with the first durian, you do the same with the second durian. Continue this process until all durians have been thus weighted (or you get crazy). For the 30 durians, you have 435 [= $(30 \times 30 - 30)/2$] pairs of such weights. You then calculated the average weight of these 435 pairs, doing this gave you a very accurate weight for the whole basket. This is analogous to the ubiquitous *Cronbach's alpha coefficient* which is an indication of *internal consistency reliability*. This coefficient indicates the extent with which students who do well in one question also tend to do well in all the remaining questions.

So far, we have been talking about score reliability applied mainly to objective questions. What about essay-type questions? Here, we are looking for *inter-rater agreement,* that is, consistency between two or among more teachers marking the same set of answer scripts.

Do you think two teachers marking the same set of answer scripts will give the same mark or at least two sets of marks that are close enough? This can be tested out by a simple small-scale experiment. And this was done many years back.

A Secondary Three student was asked to answer this question:

> *Name four vitamins and give a detailed account of the sources and functions of each. In each case, say if they can be stored in the body, and whether they are affected by heat.*

Copies were then made of his answer and given to 43 experienced teachers to mark, with this instruction:

> Give an overall rating to the answer using excellent, good, average, weak, or poor. Also, give a mark between 0 and 30 (full mark) with 15 (50%) as the passing mark.

The results are rather disconcerting. No teachers rated this one and the same answer as either excellent or poor. Twelve teachers rated it as good, 29 as average, and two as weak. What is even more disturbing is that the lowest mark awarded is 12 and the highest 22.5, with a difference of 10.5 marks for the same answer! At the same time, those 12 teachers who rated the answer as *good* gave marks ranging from 20 to 22.5. Another 29 teachers who rated the answer as *average* gave marks ranging from 13 to 22. At the other end, two teachers who rated it *weak* gave marks from 12 to 15.

So, is the answer good, average, or poor? How good is good, average, and poor in terms of marks? Obviously, this is where all great minds do not think alike since there is very little agreement among the 43 teachers marking one and the same answer to an essay-type question on scientific facts!

You may think that this just happens by chance. No. Findings like this have been repeatedly found with different groups of teachers. Moreover, American and British research over the past century or so shows such inconsistency to be rampant. There are many reasons accounting for this upsetting phenomenon. What worries us is that such lack of inter-rater agreement (reliability) leads to wrong decisions. In the Singapore context of high-stakes exams, this is all the more important as we use exams for classification, and wrong decisions lead to waste of human resources and training facilities to the disadvantage of our social and economic developments. [10]

Validity

If an exam is meant to assess the children' mathematical abilities, then it should actually measure such abilities and nothing else. The same goes for all other subjects. *Validity* is the technical term used for discussing how well a set of exam results is actually reflecting whatever it is designed to measure. Defining validity like this may sound like a dog chasing its own tail, but we can't help it because of the complex nature of the concept of validity.

Let's say you are interested in your height and not your weight. You continue to use the bathroom scale for this purpose. You step on it and the dial shows 65 kg and you then call this *65 cm*! Even you do this several times and get more or less the same reading of 65, the scores are perfectly reliable. But, we know that they are totally wrong as indications of your height.

The reason is simple because a scale is designed to measure weight but not height. In technical terms, a scale does not serve as a valid instrument for measuring height — a function it is not meant for. When you use a tape-ruler to measure the distance from the sole of your feet to the top of your head, you will get a totally different reading which truly indicates your height. In short, a scale does not give valid information of your height. This sound too obvious but confusion between reliability and validity can often be found even among professionals and we need be wary of it.

How, then, can the validity of a set of exam scores be checked? There are quite a number of ways and we shall focus only on just a few practical ones in the school context, where students' performance is concerned.

First, teachers designing exams need be concerned with *face validity*. Simply said, this means a Mathematics test must look like a Mathematics test, having many numbers appearing among the questions asking for calculation and problem solving. It is difficult to imagine a Mathematics test with no numbers and does not ask children to do some calculation and solve some story-problems. Likewise, a Language exam ought to have questions assessing vocabulary, grammar, punctuation, sentence making, etc., which are typical language abilities. The same goes for Science and other subjects. All in all, an exam of any subject must look like what it is supposed to look like and this is its face validity.

More importantly, the items of the test must be set with close proximity to the topics and complexity as stipulated by the relevant syllabus for the class level. This is the *content validity* which is the most critical for attainment test if the assessment is to truly reflect the students' learning of a subject or topics within it. As illustrated by the TOS earlier, the emphasis on topics and cognitive skills need to be specified when planning such a test so that they are consistent with the objectives of teaching. This is to ensure that students are assessed on the important subject matter and the abilities of using the content knowledge, and the scores they get truly indicate whether they have learned as expected and how well they have learned.

Next, we have what is called *predictive validity*. This is the most important for exams which are used to classify and channel children. The basic assumption of streaming and tracking is that students who have done well will be able to benefit more from subsequent learning. That is to say, students with good performance in a subject earlier (say, Math at Primary Six) will do well later in the same subject (say, Math at Secondary Four). An extension of this idea is that those who do Math well at PSLE are able to do well later in GCE 'O-level and even later in GCE 'A'-level Mathematics and beyond. In technical language, the PSLE has predictive validity in forecasting future performance in Math. This is by and large the case in Singapore context and, again, is consistent with the research finding that the best single predictor for a subject is earlier performance in the same subject. [11]

Thus, if a student is good in Math now, you can be quite sure that he will be good in Math later. The same goes for the other subjects taught in school. Under the normal circumstance, this is the case, unless there is some kind of unforeseen reasons such as a change in interest, teaching, or home environment, etc.

However, there is a practical problem to rely entirely on predictive validity to assess the validity of an exam, because of the time gap, for example, from PSLE to GCE 'O-level Exam takes at least four years. Here, *concurrent validity* will help. Concurrent means 'going at the same time' and this solves the time gap problem of predictive validity. For instance, we agree that effective learning and good exam performance depend to a large extent on cognitive ability (or, use the sensitive, old-fashioned term, *intelligence*). Thus, if a student scores high on an intelligence test, you can expect him to be good in Language and Math. By extension, if the student is good in Math, he will be good in Physics. Likewise, if he scores high in Language, he is likely to score high also in History. All these are due to the common elements among intelligence, Language, Mathematics, Physics, and History.

So, when checking the validity of a Math exam, we can look at the correlation between the Math scores and intelligence test scores (IQ), or even between the Math scores and Language scores, because we are looking at concurrent validity — the correlation between two things that should by logic happen together. One caution here is that the correlation between Math and Language should not be so high that you have good reason to suspect that the Math paper is so heavily loaded with language that it practically is a language exam. This takes us to the question of biases that affects validity. Incidentally, this is the problem with the three tests of Reading, Mathematics and Science of the Programme for International Student Assessment (PISA) where the correlations are around $r = 0.95$!

Biases

Take a most unlikely situation. A teacher sets questions on only half of the topics taught — say, only the odd-numbered chapters because there is not enough time to cover all topics in the exam time (usually two hours or so). For the same reason, children find it not possible to learn well all topics, so they resort to guessing which topics the questions are likely to come from. Student A guesses correctly that the teacher will focus on the odd-numbered chapters and studies thoroughly these topics. Student B is not so fortunate; he guesses, wrongly, that questions are to come from the even-numbered chapters and studies thoroughly these chapters, ignoring the rest.

What do you think will happen? Student A gets a very high mark (almost perfect 100%) while student B a very low mark (or nearly 0%).

What then is the interpretation? Student A knows almost perfectly the subject and student B almost nothing.

Do the two marks reflect the knowledge of the two students correctly? Of course not. In fact, both know about half of the topics taught. This will show up when all topics are covered in the exam based on a properly designed TOS. The misinterpretation is the result of misleading information provided by an ill-designed TOS and the exam based on it. Here, the real difference between students A and B is their ability to guess correctly where the questions are to come from. Such ability in correct guessing is not what the exam is designed to assess. This exam is favouring student A at the expense of student B. It is biased due to poor design of the exam. Had there been proper coverage of the topics, both children are likely to get what they deserve, that is, about 50% of the marks allowed.

There are many other sources of biases. For instance, an exam consists of some 30 objective questions. When typing the answer keys into the computer, the teacher made a careless mistake by typing 'b' as the correct answer when it should be 'a'. Thus, all children who choose 'a' as the correct answer (correctly) will be marked *wrong* for this question. At the same time, all children choosing 'b' as the correct answer (wrongly) will gain one mark undeservingly. This is a *systematic* bias due to technical carelessness. The lesson is for us not to trust the computer totally. We still need to trust the human teachers and hope they are careful enough.

Bias due to human factors is not uncommon, especially when the exam results depend on the judgment of teachers. For some reasons unknown hitherto, some teachers are strict markers. When marking answers to essay-type questions, they tend to give lower marks when compared with other teachers. On the other hand, there are teachers who are rather kind to their children and tend to give higher marks when compared with others. Then, there are conservative markers who consciously or subconsciously avoid giving high or low marks. The marks they give, therefore, tend to bunch within a narrow range of the allowed range. And, this may combine with strict or lenient marking. Such idiosyncratic marker behaviour yields marks that do not truly reflect the abilities of the children. Such problems may not be very acute if the number of student is small and the same teacher marks all answers, although the validity remains questionable. In large-scale high-stakes exams where many teachers mark many different sets of answers to the same questions, such bias is worrisome because students are likely to be misclassified with all the attendant ill-effects that go with it.

On a smaller scale, a teacher, for some reasons, may be highly critical about students' handwriting. Thus, when she is not happy with a student's handwriting, she may take a few marks off from the marks he deserves. If penmanship is not part of the intended exam, doing this lowers the validity for the exam result, although the teacher may feel justified to deduct marks for poor handwriting.

For another example, several teachers mark different sets of answers to the same essay-type questions. When marking a Science exam, one teacher accepts incomplete sentences as long as the ideas are correct, but another insists that children must answer with complete sentences otherwise some marks are deducted even when the ideas are correct. In this case, the marks reflect to some extent the preferences of the two teachers. Hence, the results given by the second teacher are biased and do not indicate accurately the levels achieved by the children. The same goes for such things like spelling and punctuation, in non-language subjects.

The ideal markers are those who make full use of the allowed ranges of marks and do not have the tendency to mark too strictly or leniently. Such ideal markers are hard to find. Besides, marker idiosyncrasies are very much part of the markers' personality, culture, training, and habit and are therefore hard to get rid of.

What then can be done? A few practices have been used. First, for such minor things like accepting or penalizing incomplete sentences, as long as all markers agree on the same rules, the problem is solved. And, to be fair, such rules must be made known to the students taking the exam. Then, the use of marking scheme can reduce (though not eliminate totally) inter-rater differences. That is, when an essay question is set, the setter also lists the expected answers and specifies the marks to be awarded to each of the points in the answers. When marking, all markers follow as closely as possible the marking scheme to reduce the influence of personal preferences.

For large-scale exams involving many markers, a chief examiner arranges for all the markers to mark the same sample of answers and then compared the results. When gross differences are found, the chief examiners will consult with the deviating markers and come to a consensus as to what marks should be given. The chief examiner will also monitor every now and then for any further deviation if the marking period is extended over a few days. Doing this is to cut down individual differences among the markers so that such differences are not mistaken as individual differences of the children.

Of course, to reduce bias, there is still the proverbial model answer. For this, the question setter answers her own question. She (and other markers) then uses this model answer against which all students' answers are compared. Answers closer to the model get higher marks and those different from it lower marks. This sounds great, but read a true story.

A professor marked a large pile of papers using his model answer. In the old days when air-con was not available (even to a professor!) and electric fan was the only way to keep cool. (By the way, understandably, teachers can get very heated when marking papers, especially the poor ones.) Half way, he went for a tea break (not coffee break because this happened in UK). When he returned, he found the papers all over the floor. He also could not find the model answer. This was not a problem since he had marked so many of the papers and had a good idea of what should be the ideal answer. So, he continued with the unenviable task and completed marking.

All papers had been marked and the next step was to enter marks into the mark sheet. He religiously entered the marks according to the index numbers (all important exams conceal student identities this way). He then came across a poor answer which deserved a poor mark and it had no index number — what a careless student. He put it aside and continues with the rest. At the end, he found all names had marks. Whose was the one without an index number? And, it was failed!

Consequences

Not so long ago, assessment experts talk about *consequential* validity. Test scores are used to make important decisions such as streaming and selection. Such decisions have critical consequences to student's opportunity to learn and develop further. These consequences have implications for both the individuals' and the nation's developments. It does not take much imagination to think of how a wrong decision in selection can adversely affect the life chance of a deserving student and the availability of a potential talent to the nation. A wrong decision in such a case is in fact a double loss: when a more deserving student is rejected, a less deserving one takes his place.

Students who do well in the PSLE are considered to be capable of benefiting from the next high level of learning, that is, secondary education. Likewise, GCE-'O' performance is used to decide who goes to junior colleges for learning at the GCE-'A' level or the polytechnic for practical training. There may be (and bound to have, because of the fallible exam results) some cases of misclassification or wrong identification. There are cases of those who have passed the PSLE not doing well in 'O'-level four years later and some who have done well at 'O'-level not doing well at 'A'-level. Conversely, there are students who do not do well enough at 'O"-level to get the chance to learn at 'A'-level, but they may do well enough at 'A'-level if given a chance to try.

Let's do a mind experiment (Albert Einstein always did this). If the predictor scores (of, say, PSLE) have a perfect correlation with the criterion scores (of, say, 'O'-level), then all who pass in the former will also pass in the latter, and vice versa, if *all* PSLE candidates are allowed to go to secondary schools (this, of course, is not the practice). Then, the validity coefficient is 1.00 showing a perfect prediction.

However, in contrast, as is true of all exams, the prediction is never perfect and a validity coefficient of 0.80 is normally expected. In this case, if all PSLE candidates are allowed to go to secondary schools and take the 'O'-level four years later, some who should have passed may fail and some others who should fail may pass. These two groups show the inconsistency in prediction due to lack of perfect prediction.

To use medical jargons, those who passed earlier but failed later are the *false positives*. On the other hand, those who failed earlier but given the chance and made it later are the *misses* (or, *false negatives*). Medically speaking, false positives are patients diagnosed as having a disease but in fact do not have it, and misses are the opposite cases. Both are results of inaccurate diagnosis which is yet to be a perfect science. Likewise, in law, there are cases of innocent people wrongly condemned to jail for years for crimes they did not commit before the actual offenders came out to publicly confess their crimes. Conversely, there are also cases where actual criminals were set free because of insufficient or erroneous evidence.

If this is the case for medicine and law, it is not reasonable to assume or expect perfect prediction in education where assessments are far from being perfect. Fortunately, such cases are not many and it shows that the PSLE and GCE-'O' exams have consequential validity. Should there be a large number of false positives and misses, the consequential validity of these two high-stakes exams will be suspect. Of course, the rare cases, of an N-course student getting a PhD and another EM3 student granted a scholarship to study, both in the London University, attest to the fallibility of assessment as is currently practised. Here, the probability of error is low but the possibility is real.

One contributing factor to the high predictive and consequential validities of the PSLE, the GCE-'O' and the GCE-'A' exam is the highly similar modes of learning required throughout the whole system from primary, through secondary and pre-university, to university level. What students do well when young they also do well when grown up, provided the environment does not change.

Another contributing factor is that students are mainly assessed through paper-and-pencil tests at these levels. What may happen beyond? Well, it depends. Since junior college students good in science are most likely to opt for a science degree at the university, the knowledge base is there and the modes of learning do not change drastically, they are likely to do well in the sciences. The same goes for other degrees. This, of course, is the system perpetuating itself. Thus, in terms of degree-level performance, the GCE-'A' performance has consequential validity as long as the modes of learning at the two levels remain highly similar. The world of work after university demands very different kind of abilities beyond book-learning and university grades (GPA or grade-point average) may not be a good predictor of job performance.

Why some bright children do not do well?

There are a small number of cases where highly promising undergraduates disappoint their parents and professors with less than expected performance. Does this show that the GCE-'A' performance having low predictive and consequential validity? Maybe — and maybe not. There are possible statistical and psychological reasons to explain this unhappy situation.

First is the statistical explanation. Ours is a highly selective system. Thus, the higher we go the narrow the range of test scores. For instance, at the primary level, there is a full range of 'normal' intelligence, except the low intelligence scores that classify some unfortunate children as mentally retarded or slow learners. As a cohort of children move from primary school through secondary school to junior college, the less intelligent children (who do not do too well in exams) leave school on their own accord or are not given the opportunity of moving up the educational ladder. The obvious consequence of this is the narrower range of intelligence as the level goes higher. It can be inferred from the normal curve of intelligence test scores that those who are admitted to the university have IQ 115 on average. Since IQ 115 is the point one SD above the mean 100 of the IQ distribution, it separates the top 16% from the remaining 84%.

The narrower range (technically called *truncated distribution*) is the problem, because correlation depends on the ranges of the two sets of scores used for calculating this vital statistic. With such a narrower range of IQ, the correlation is under-estimated. Therefore, within the university, IQ or 'A'-level grades may not be effective in predicting academic performance — a statistical artefact. This naturally leads to the conclusion that intelligence and academic ability are not enough; it take something more to do well in the university. And, what is that *something*?

Next is the psychological explanation. Since undergraduates are all high-IQ children and the range of their IQs will be rather narrow, they cannot compete on IQ and earlier achievement because of the truncated distributions. Their personality, motivation, attitude and, to some extent, modes of learning begin to play a more critical role. In other words, at this high level of learning, it is not only the intelligence that counts, the affective or emotional aspects of the students play an important or even critical role in academic success.

Besides these, the university students are young adults and have to contend with normal personal (e.g., the match or the lack of it between aspiration and programme) and social problems (e.g., boy-girl relationship) of becoming full-fledged adults, in addition to the rather heavy demands of learning at the university level. These problems will interfere with their learning when not properly resolved. When this unfortunately happens, it is not the lack of predictive or consequential validity of the exams, and not doing well is not the culprit of failure but a symptom indicating unsolved life problems.

Relation between reliability and validity

In assessment parlance, it is always said that reliability is a *necessary but not sufficient* condition of validity. In other words, a set of test scores should be reliable before they can be valid; they may be reliable but may and may not be valid at the same time. This can be put in yet another way, that is, the scores must assess the ability or knowledge of interest consistently before we can be sure they might be assessing what they are meant to assess.

Imagine a shooter whose bullets always land on the same spot but not on the bull's eye. His shooting is highly reliable (consistent) but not valid for the purpose of shooting (hitting the target). Likewise, whatever a perpetual liar says is highly reliable but not valid, because he always lies and you just cannot trust him. If you have a damaged bathroom scale, it gives you the same body weight consistently, but all the readings are not valid since they do not truly reflect health condition.

Improving reliability and ensuring validity are very time-consuming effort and require technical competencies in terms of familiarity with the syllabus, ability in choosing the right item formats, writing effective questions, and conducting some statistical analysis. Until such time when all teachers are equipped with all these knowledge and skills, we need to be aware of the probable pitfalls of assessment and be cautious when interpreting results obtained through tests and exams. At least, do not blame the student when it is not his fault that he does not score high because of the less than desired quality of the exams.

9. Preparing for Exams and Coping with Exam Stress

Now, we are back to square one — Why have assessment, exams, and tests? To recall, exams and tests are tools teachers use to get information on students' learning (or the lack of it), that is, assessment.

The information gathered with these tools is useful to the children to show them where they have done well, where they could have done better, and where their effort should be focused on before the next testing. It is also useful to the teacher so that she knows the strengths and weaknesses of the class as a whole and the students as individuals, what difficulties there are, and what needs be done to help the students further. The information is, of course, of interest to school leaders who are concerned about their students' performance. It assures them that things are alright and alert them to where attention is warranted. Besides, assessment results are useful for grouping and selecting students for further teaching and special training.

Taking body weight, under the normal circumstance, should not be a cause of concern. However, anxiety arises when going to the clinic for a physical check-up when body weight is usually taken as a routine. Likewise, exams are a normal part of teaching and learning and should not cause concern. Nonetheless, because many of the exams are high-stakes assessment, teachers and school leaders naturally become more anxious than usual when there is an impending national exam. And, because of this, students may also become more anxious than usual. As for the teachers, the students' exam performance indirectly reflect their teaching effectiveness, and this has a bearing on their end-of-year performance evaluation. As for the school leaders, results of nation-level exams are always associated with the school's reputation which they care about.

Here, we will leave the anxiety of the parents, school leaders, and teachers to themselves but focus on the students' exam anxiety.

Exam anxiety

Let's make a simple calculation. Assuming there are four bi-weekly tests for four core subjects, two semester assessments in two semesters, one mid-year exam, and one end-of-year exam. How many exams a student has to take from Primary One to Secondary Four? At least, three hundred! Isn't it strange that with such an extensive experience in taking exams, students may still be anxious when exams are looming. Moreover, unfortunately, some students who are well prepared may not remember what they have learned when writing the papers — the mind just goes blank!

Anxiety has been an important area of psychological research as it impinges on many aspects of the lives of people. Exam anxiety is a special topic in the education context and is created by education itself. People become anxious when they face uncertainty and feel threatened. When people are anxious, their mental and physical functions are likely to be less efficient than what they should be, and disturbing thoughts interfere with the normal thinking processes. Recall your own experience when you sat behind the wheel for the very first time to learn driving or when you were waiting to be interviewed for a coveted job. That's anxiety.

Students are also people. They too can become anxious when facing uncertainty (*Will I do well in the exam next week?*) and feel threatened (*What will my mum say and do should I fail to get the marks she wants?*). Such uncertainty and threats lower their capabilities in preparing for and taking the exams. They divide their attention between preparing for the exams and worrying about the consequences. Naturally, a student in this position is less effective than he used to be.

Psychologists recognize two different though related types of anxiety — *trait anxiety* and *state anxiety*. We may not like it, but some students are born and have learned to be more anxious when compared with other children. This tendency to be more anxious than others becomes a characteristic of such children and is a trait of their personalities. Children with trait anxiety will show shyness, withdrawal, tension, or even aggression and related symptoms in many normal situations, especially unfamiliar or totally new ones in which other children will behave as if there is nothing unusual. This will not be further discussed as it falls within the realm of personality psychology and hence is beyond the scope of this book.

On the other hand, children who are normally not anxious about many normal things in daily life may suddenly become anxious with the thought of an impending exam. This emotional reaction is aroused only in connection with assessment and nothing else. This is a special kind of anxiety — state anxiety. Because it is temporary or situation-specific, hence *state* to differentiate it from *trait* anxiety.

How do children acquire state anxiety for exams? When children first attend school, they take exams as just another boring activity they have to go through. Whatever the exam results are, they are of little interest — nothing to worry about if poor and nothing to brag about when good. When Samuel topped his class in overall and in Math of all Primary One classes at the end of his first school year, it was more exciting to his parents than anyone else. When asked, *"Samuel, are you the first in your class?"* He answered *"yes"* in a matter-of-fact manner with no emotional signs at all.

Over months and years, parents invest their emotions in their children's exam results. In short, children's marks are always followed by emotional reactions (and in most cases, over-reactions) from the parents. As is said, practice makes perfect. Through such regular practice, children learn to see exams in an emotional way rather than taking them as per normal. Thus children not only learn knowledge and skills and taking exams, they also learn to react to assessment in an emotional way. And, the negative emotional way shows up as exam anxiety — *state anxiety* associated with exams. Likewise, teachers may react emotionally to children's poor or lower than expected assessment results. This impacts on the students just like the parents' negative reaction does. In short, parents and teachers *teach* children to feel anxious about exams; exam anxiety is what children learn from the emotional reaction of their parents and teachers.

Signs of exam anxiety

When people have become unusually anxious, they behave differently from how they have been doing. Teachers and parents who have children experiencing exam anxiety need be aware of some common signs or symptoms of anxiety before helping them cope with it. Here is something to watch out for but the list is not exhaustive.

One common anxiety indicator is avoiding friends and keeping away from school activities of personal preference. Although a student's friendships and interest are fleeting, especially if he is rather young, a sudden change with no obvious reasons signifies the high probability of anxiety being experienced. Why this is so is not certain. Perhaps, he needs to be alone to cool himself, perhaps he does not want people to unwittingly touch on his soft spot; perhaps, anxiety is so acute that it generalizes (spreads) over to non-threatening situations such as friends and fond games.

Another common anxiety indicator is the inability to think. Uncontrolled or uncontrollable anxiety disrupts the normal mental functioning and diverts attention from what it should be focused on. Thus, a boy overly anxious about the next exam will not be able to concentrate on studying but keeps thinking about the possibility of doing badly (and disappointing his mother), though not necessarily failing it! In an extreme situation, he may just refuse to study any more, believing that there is no chance of reaching the goal and hence no point studying.

Fight and flight are two normal ways people react to unusual frustration and threats. The same go for children, perhaps even more since they have not learned to disguise. When the exam is seen by a child as overwhelming, he may just give up trying. And, since exam involves his ego (self-concept), he sees himself as a failure even before trying. He, then, needs to resolve the emotional imbalance by taking it out on others through showing anger or demeaning himself as a useless person. Hence, sudden anger or crying is symptomatic of exam anxiety.

Another common sign of exam anxiety is the loss of appetite or vomiting after food. Growing children love to eat and they need to eat a lot to grow. When they become overly anxious about exams, their normal digestive processes are disturbed just like worrying adults losing interest in food. This is a normal reaction of the body (or rather the nervous systems) to anxiety arousing experience, but it is not normal for children to be in such a situation for exams.

Exam anxiety may disturb children's sleep. Such disturbances may show up as insomnia or nightmares. Both are not good for the growing children who should be sleeping soundly to be healthy. Such unpleasant symptoms could be seen as the problems experienced during the waking hours 'sinking deeper' into the subconscious and may make things worse in the longer run.

On the other hand, ironically, over-sleeping or sleeping much longer than usual could be another sign of exam anxiety. Since the waking hours are painful because of the thought of possible failure, sleeping over it is an escape from or defence against the psychological pain. Yet another defence is indulging in daydreaming or fantasy, imaging passing the tests with flying colour or doing very well in some other more interesting activities. Whatever it may be, both are unrealistic reactions to what should be a normal challenge.

People do not change their characters or personalities abruptly without reasons, although people may change imperceptibly over a long period of time. People's sudden changes in characters and personalities manifest through sudden changes in behavior toward themselves, people around them, and activities they previously like. In short, the person, as we sometimes say, *is not himself.* A usually active student may suddenly become very subdued, and vice versa. He may become unfriendly or over-friendly. He may not want to do things he spent lots of time in the past. Should these happen and the exam is drawing near, these could signify that he is experiencing acute exam anxiety.

Although all the symptoms described above are not specific to exam anxiety, they are symptoms of anxiety nonetheless, especially when they precede exams. Should they occur and no exam is nearing, the anxiety could be due to other aspects of school life or family life and the problems need be identified and attended to.

Anxiety and achievement

Lest you get the impression that anxiety is always bad, let's look at what psychology called the *Yerkes-Dodson Law.* This scientific law is based on the research on the relation between arousal and performance in cognition by R. M. Yerkes and J. D. Dodson as early as 1908. If you draw a big U and turn it upside down, what you see is the famous Yerkes-Dodson Curve. This inverted U-curve seems a good representation of the findings of many studies on the relationship between motivation (arousal) and performance. [12]

Common sense says, the stronger the motivation, the better the performance. Wrong! The relationship between the two cannot be represented by a southwest-to-northeast straight line. Research consistently shows that the relationship is better depicted as the inverted U-curve, what technically called curvilinear relationship. And, what does this mean?

According to the Yerkes-Dodson Law, when motivation increases, performance also improves, *but only up to a point*. Beyond this point, stronger motivation begins to be detrimental to performance causing poorer and not better result. Thus, the learning curve becomes an inverted U. Applying this principle to exam anxiety, we can say that some degree of exam anxiety is useful to motivate a student to perform better, but too much anxiety will be harmful to learning. Why should this be?

When a boy is not sufficiently motivated, he does not care much about exam results, and so he will not put in the necessary effort to do well and the performance cannot be good. On the other hand, when the anxiety is too strong, it competes for his attention and mental energy and therefore interferes with thinking processes that exam requires, resulting in poorer performance. Thus, it is the optimal level of motivation (anxiety) that is best for performance.

The problem here is how much anxiety is optimal? This depends on the individual children. Each student, because of his personality and experience, has his own optimal motivation level. What is too much for one student may be too little for another. Here, the teachers and parents have an important role to play. Through daily interactions in class and at home, teachers and parents will have ample opportunity to observe how the children react to the teacher's and parents' efforts to motivate them and adjust the level accordingly.

Preparing for exams physically and emotionally

It is a truism that a healthy mind goes with a healthy body. A student who is physically weak cannot be expected to do well in school work, especially during the stressful exam period. So, for a student to do well in exams, he needs to be physically fit. This means eating right in the first place. Studies show that after a fat-rich meal, people tended to be slow in thinking. How you feel and think after a heavy meal? Regular physical activities not only make the child's body healthy but also give his mind a chance to rest and recover from mental fatigue. Then, there is his all-important sleep. Assessment is mentally demanding and requires concentration. When a child does not sleep well, he is tired and finds it difficult to focus his thinking, not to say he feels sleepy at the wrong time and in the wrong place. Then, a vicious circle may set in between tiredness and sleeplessness, affecting his performance when taking an exam.

Since preparing for exam is a highly demanding task to most children, it dulls their minds imperceptibly. This is where the 'diminishing return' principle sets in. In other words, the longer the student spends preparing for exam, there will be a time when his mind is so tired that it does not work as effectively and efficiently as before. Before this happens, it is wise for him to take a rest or, preferably, have a diversion — do something other than studying. This gives him a break from the monotonous task and the anxious feeling. Games, chit-chatting, singing, listening to music, watching a TV programme, etc. etc., and even just eating or drinking something may be the much needed diversion. The whole idea is to relax and go for a change.

These things happen in the child's home where the teacher is not there to do anything. However, teachers can talk to and remind their students about keeping fit in preparation for impending exams, especially the high-stakes ones. Teachers can also advise the students' parents about this when the occasion arises. School leaders may organize talks on such topics for parents perhaps through the parents' help groups of their schools.

Preparing the student mentally

The Scout's motto *Be Ready* is most appropriate for exam preparation. If a student cares enough about the impending exam, he feels ready for it. The best way to prepare a student for it is to have him mentally well-prepared. As the old Chinese saying goes, *Repair the roof before it rains*. How?

It is obvious that long before the exam, the student needs to revise what he has been taught and will be assessed on. Thus, he needs to develop a habit of active learning, making learning his business. When he has acquired the habit of regular revision and feels responsible for his own learning, he will also build up his confidence because this reduces the sense of uncertainty and urgency, and results become more predictable in his mind.

In order to achieve this sense of control, the student needs to plan his revision and study with a regular timetable. Here is where the teacher and parent can greatly help children to plan and ensure time is properly allotted to the various subjects with more time for his difficult subjects. When planning a revision timetable, make sure that similar subjects do not come next to one another; it is more effective if there is a change between different subjects in succession — language-math-language-science sequence is better than language-language-science-math, etc. The switch from one subject to a different subject makes the mind feel fresh and work more effectively. It also minimizes what psychologists of learning call *interference* or *negative transfer* when similar but different things are learned in close succession.

The student also needs to learn how to effectively learn. Rote learning or sheer memorization is not helpful. These are modes of learning children resort to only when the learning materials are meaningless or very difficult to them. Always help the student to relate what he is to learn now with what he has learned before — looking for links, meanings, contrasts, comparisons, and other ways that the materials can be organized under some headings. Also, encourage the student to draw pictures, diagrams, and mind-maps to represent the ideas. Another helpful technique is to have the student ask himself questions and try to answer them. The Chinese word for scholarship (xuewen) in fact is made up of two Chinese characters: xue (to learn) and *wen* (to ask), meaning to learn is to ask questions.

Developing good exam-taking habits is also important. This is an area where the teacher is of great help. First, encourage your students to guess as best they can when they comes across something they do not know too well. Some people disagree with this, believing that guessing lead to more mistakes. But, then, in daily life, we do not always have the full knowledge we need and we have to guess in order to answer a question or solve a problem. Even scientists have to guess as best they can by making hypothesis based on currently available *partial* knowledge. Guessing allow the student to use his partial knowledge and develop the ability of predicting. This is not uneducational, on the contrary, it is more educational than trying to remember and then regurgitate. The ability to guess using partial knowledge is a useful ability when taking an exam.

Train your student to write legibly, but not necessarily 'beautifully' (whatever this means). Neat and legible writing show clarity of the answers and are more pleasant to the teacher who has a whole lot of papers to mark. Illegible and messy handwriting cannot be clearly read in the first place and they upset the busy teachers, too. These are more likely to lead to poorer marks — how do you expect the teacher to award marks when she can't even be sure what has been written?

Train your student to check his work every time he has completed some parts of the exam. This is an important, good exam-taking habit. Remembering a correct answer after leaving the exam room is definitely too late. It is better to be sure than sorry. The student need not work fast but he needs to work carefully. Thus, train him to cheek his own work to avoid carelessness that always leads to losing marks.

If assessment results are important, you may wish to use the *Assessment Preparedness Scale* to help the students. The profiles can be used for discussion with the students individually or in groups and can be repeated, say, every half a year. The scale may be used for study in general or with a specific subject in view. This, in a way, is exam-training.

Assessment Preparedness Scale

Think of your study habits. Ask yourself whether each of the descriptions below describes you and how well. Use the following ratings.

4 = Very true   3 = Mostly true   2 = Often true   1 = Occasionally true

1. I am well and fit and do not take MCs.	4 3 2 1
2. I have an excellent attendance record.	4 3 2 1
3. I do my homework punctually.	4 3 2 1
4. I need no prompting to study.	4 3 2 1
5. I talk to friends about tests and homework.	4 3 2 1
6. I keep records of my test results.	4 3 2 1
7. I like to solve problems on my own.	4 3 2 1
8. I try to find a way out when faced with difficulty.	4 3 2 1
9. I am *not* put off when something unexpected happens.	4 3 2 1
10. I start revision for assessment ahead of time.	4 3 2 1
11. I have a timetable for revision.	4 3 2 1
12. I have formed a study group for assessment.	4 3 2 1
13. I set myself questions when revising.	4 3 2 1
14. I draw diagrams and pictures to help me remember.	4 3 2 1
15. I link one idea to relevant ideas in my revision.	4 3 2 1
16. I receives good comments from teachers for my work.	4 3 2 1
17. I always scores 75% or higher in tests.	4 3 2 1
18. I do well in most subjects.	4 3 2 1
19. I am good at guessing the correct answers.	4 3 2 1
20. I write neatly and my handwriting is easy to read.	4 3 2 1
21. I am careful to check my work before handing it in.	4 3 2 1

Now, you have done your self-rating, it is time to draw your *Assessment Preparedness Profile.*

1. Add up the total scores for each set of questions according to the numbers below.
2. Circle the appropriate numbers in the right-hand block.
3. Draw lines linking one circle to the next to get the profile.
4. Find the grand total score.

		Assessment Preparedness Profile								
Aspects	Questions	High			Moderate			Low		
Regular study	*1–3*	12	11	10	9	8	7	6	5	4	3
Self-motivation	*4–6*	12	11	10	9	8	7	6	5	4	3
Confidence	*7–9*	12	11	10	9	8	7	6	5	4	3
Planning	*10–12*	12	11	10	9	8	7	6	5	4	3
Study skills	*13–15*	12	11	10	9	8	7	6	5	4	3
Competence	*16–18*	12	11	10	9	8	7	6	5	4	3
Test-taking	*19–21*	12	11	10	9	8	7	6	5	4	3

The profile you have just drawn shows where your strengths are and where you needs more guidance. What about your grand total score? Where does the score place you on the scale below?

Not well-prepared at all	Not well-prepared	Reasonably well-prepared	Very well-prepared
21–28	29–49	50–70	71–84

10. How Is Creativity Assessed?

Creativity! Creativity! Creativity!

In recent years, the word *creativity* has become a buzzword in Singapore. You find it in the newspapers, in TV news, at seminars, in public talks, etc., etc., even in daily conversions. Everyone is using the phrase *thinking out of the box* as if there are no other creative ways to describe creative thinking. Why are we crazy about creativity? What is creativity? What is creativity in the school context? And, more importantly, how is creativity assessed?

Before we talk about the assessment of creativity, we need to understand what creative products are and how people, adults and children alike, create. Above all, what a creative student looks like. These are all relevant to the school leaders, teachers, and parents because of their common interest in the children under their care.

What is a creative product?

Would you like to carry a heavy tape-recorder while jogging at the East Coast Park? Sony's boss Akio Morita was a jogger and a music lover at the same time, but he couldn't do both before his own invention. One day, while jogging in the park, an idea came to his mind — *Can't I reduce the clumsy, heavy tape-recorder to something I can carry along so that I can enjoy music while jogging?* He told his engineers his idea. They listened very politely as all Japanese subordinates did and kept saying "Hi! Hi!", although they said to themselves in their minds, *"Who on earth will buy a tape-recorder that looks more like a toy?"*

But, Morita persisted and the engineers just had to do the silly thing the boss asked for. Months later, the first Walkman was born, and, amazingly, it soon became the toy of many young people around the world. The once omnipresent Walkman was later replaced by iPod. By now, even Zen Pod has been overtaken by MP3. What next? That is creativity. Incidentally, there was a 20-year lawsuit between Sony and a German inventor Andreas Pavel over the patent right of Walkman, and Sony paid millions of dollars to settle the case.

Would you like to buy a bottle of glue that does not stick! Arthus L. Fry was commissioned to develop stronger glue. He needed a container and could not find one nearby. He went into the storeroom to get a used container. He picked one from the shelf among many discarded, unsuccessful trials. Fry snatched a little of what was in the can and ground it between his thumb and finger and found it not sticky at all. Suddenly, an idea came to his mind. He had seen his colleagues pinning small notes on to the cupboard doors, the partitions, etc., and made ugly looking pinholes all over the places. He went to his desk, cut some papers into stripes, rubbed a little of the non-sticky glue to them. He then gave these to his friends to use as 'reminders'. They liked it so much and asked for more. The 3M notepads were born. Nowadays, we can buy 3M Post-it notes of different sizes, shapes, and colours in bookshops everywhere. And, most important, the glue that is not sticky has become a multimillion business.

These are two examples of 'small' creative ideas that later turned into gigantic businesses. There are many, many stories like these, such as those of Xerox, Polaroid, and Nike. Somebody has crazy ideas and then something unheard of, disbelieved (or even laughed at) and unimportant came into existence because of the craziness. Of course, there are more important inventions that did not happen by chance but with purposes — the splitting of atom making possible the atomic bomb that changed the history of human race, for instance, and of course, the computer link-ups that became the ubiquitous Internet that has penetrated all walls of schools, banks, offices, homes, etc. wherever there are people working or playing.

Such creative products or inventions, big or small, change the ways we live, the ways we work, and the ways we relate to and think of other people. Creative products are what people normally talk about when they think of creativity. Creative products may come in different sizes, shapes, and colours, but they have two characteristics in common.

First, for something to be considered creative, it must be new, unique, unusual, unprecedented, in a sense, surprising. Although a must, this quality of being surprising can work against creativity. In history, there have been many cases of creative ideas and their actualizations (the creative products based on the creative ideas) being laughed at and rejected when they first appeared. When the first personal computer was first invented, the IBM boss said the whole world needed only five computers.

The second characteristic of a creative product (and its idea) is its usefulness. It must fit into a problem situation or meeting a need. When the first locomotive was demonstrated, someone laughed at it and said, *"Who will ever travel in such a monster?"* The problem here is that people may not be aware of their own needs or problems. This leads to the quote attributed to Albert Einstein, *Creativity is seeing what everyone sees and thinking what none has ever thought of.*

In the context of school and classroom, we do not expect children to come up with earth-shaking ideas and products. Children's creative ideas and products come in the form of they doing something surprising and fitting — ways of solving a mathematic problem, writing a poem, drawing a picture, playing a game, singing a song, and dancing a dance, etc., etc.

What are creative processes?

If children are not expected to come up with earth-shaking ideas and products, what then is the value of developing creativity in them? In a way, this is the real spirit of education — developing students in such a way that they have a high chance of becoming creative when they grow up. This means that they must be trained in creative processes. In other words, it is not important that children produce creative things and ideas now, but it is important that they learn the processes that will equip them to create and want to create in the future. Again, in the education parlance, it is the process and not the product that counts. The interest is not on what children produce now but how they produce.

When Samuel was given a Lego helicopter, he played with it the way it was meant to be played (i.e., *following the rules*), making all sorts of movements and noises a helicopter normally makes. The next day, the helicopter disappeared and was nowhere to be seen (i.e., *breaking away from the past*). The blades, the wheels, and the body of the helicopter all had disintegrated into bits and pieces of Lego. Soon, there are a new airplane, a submarine, a truck, etc. (i.e, new products). In short, the helicopter has been first disintegrated and then transformed into something quite different. These are the outcomes of taking apart; some people call this *creative destruction* or *destructive creation*, re-combining, dropping a piece here, and adding another there. It is his way of playing creatively.

The saying that there is nothing new under the sun is in a sense very true where creativity is concerned. Creative processes involves creating something new out of something old (not from nothing to something, as many people have mistakenly thought). Creative processes are the ways by which something is re-shaped into something new, some things usually not linked are joined together, and something is given a new explanation. Of course, it is not possible to see what goes on in a child's mind when he is creating something new from something old. To understand this, we need to go back to the creative product. Thus, by looking at the new product and compared it with the old one, we can infer that the child has used one of the many creative processes.

In the classroom context, for instance, when a student reads a few sentences of the same structure, he becomes aware that the words are arranged in a certain manner and they seem to have different functions. Here, he learns about the grammar of that language. Now, if he takes one word from each group and forms a new sentence and yet another new sentence, he is not learning a language but creating it! Here, he is doing what is called morphological analysis, an important creative process used by designers of all sorts. Take another example, when given a price list from a supermarket, the boy imagines that he is helping the mother at shopping and works out the amount she has to pay and the change she should get, he is not only learning mathematics but creating it. Here, he is involved in some important creative processes — combining, re-arranging, and put-to-other uses.

Creative person

If for children creative products are not materially important, and if creative processes are somewhat nebulous, how do you find out whether a boy is creative?

Parents are so used to look at products (e.g., interesting compositions written with no grammatical and spelling mistakes, complex mathematical problems correctly solved, etc.) as evidence of learning, they tend to also look for (and be proud of) creative products of their children. This leads them to neglect the personal characteristics of creative children. If education is to develop children, as it always claims, then, parents should pay more attention to identifying creative children.

In fact, many years back American research shows that creative children are not welcome by their teachers. In a study, senior high students were tested for intelligence and creativity. They were then classified into four groups — high-intelligence-high-creativity, low-intelligence-low-creativity, low-intelligence-high-creativity, and high-intelligence-low-creativity. Teachers were asked to indicate how much they liked each of these students and to give their reasons. The children were also asked to nominate classmates they liked best and disliked most and to give reasons, too. This finding has been replicated. [13]

The results show that the teachers liked best those students in the high-intelligence-low-creativity group. Surprisingly, they did not like students high in both intelligence and creativity! One common reason for disliking high-creativity children (even if they were highly intelligent) was that such children were troublesome; one of the reasons was that they asked unusual questions and thereby disrupted the lessons. As for the classmates, creative classmates were seen as *showing off* and *trying to be smart*. Such responses of the teachers and students are understandable.

Creative children may ask questions the teachers have not prepared for and, perhaps, there is no way the teacher can prepare the answer since there may be none. Such unprepared questions are a threat to the self-respect of any conscientious teacher. Moreover, deviating from the lesson strand by asking unexpected and puzzling questions, the creative students hold back the class. Of course, the teacher who has a syllabus to cover and the other children who have a test to prepare for will not like it. Thus, it seems that having a creative student may not be a good thing!

Imagine that you are teaching about light in a Physics lessons. Then, a boy stands up and asks, *"If I ride on a beam of light travelling in the space, will there be a time when I move faster than light?"* The textbook does not have the answer and you have never thought of such a weird question. How would you feel inside you and how would you respond? The silly or funny boy named Albert Einstein asked this question. Fortunate for us, he did not ask his teacher but asked himself. And, that is the germane idea that led to the Theory of Relativity.

What then are the personal characteristics of creative children? For these, we need to go to the creativity researcher E. P. Torrance who authored the much used *Torrance Tests of Creative Thinking*. He found, during the time he was a secondary school English Language teacher, a small number of adolescents who 'did not fit' into classroom situations like the others. He noticed that these adolescents showed characteristics that set them apart from others. The ten most common of such characteristics are:

- Delight in deep thinking
- Tolerate mistakes
- Love their work
- Have clear purpose
- Enjoy their work
- Feel comfortable as a minority of one
- Are different
- Are not well-rounded
- Have a sense of mission
- Have the courage to be creative

In want of a better word, Torrance called them the *Beyonders*, meaning that these adolescents were not within the normal characterization of adolescents. Many years later when they were young adults, Torrance contacted them for information of their developments. These *Beyonders*, when compared with their normal peers, had more creative achievements the society valued in science and in arts, scholarships, and in business. Torrance's research suggests that the future developments of creative minds can be detected as early as in the secondary years if we look out for the above characteristics. What Torrance found as the characteristics could serve as the basis of assessment of creativity when they are re-cast in the form of an observation scale for use by school leaders, teachers, and parents. One such scale is appended here later. [14]

Personal and cultural creativity

The words *creative* and *creativity* have been used rather freely with almost anything somewhat unusual or not usually done, in spite of their doubtful quality of usefulness. Perhaps, in our zest to encourage creativity, we have been erroneously over-generous. Creativity researchers are in one mind that there are two levels of creativity — personal creativity and cultural creativity.

When a person does something surprising and fitting that he has *never done previously*, he shows *personal creativity,* if that is new in his personal history though it has been done by other people many times. In short, to him it is new and useful but to the society it is nothing unusual. When children are said to be creative because they draw interesting pictures or sing songs in unusual way, it is personal creativity for the simple reason that the pictures and songs are not likely to be surprising and fitting in the context of the histories of the art and music.

In contrast, when a scientist creates a new way of curing diseases that has a wide impact on human societies, it changes the way we think and act — this is *cultural creativity*. For instance, Edward Janner's 1796 'invention' of smallpox vaccine and Ian Fleming's 1928 discovery of penicillin. Likewise, when Pablo Picasso broke away from the tradition and painted with a style that allowed overlapping perspectives, he shocked the world of art, and painting did not have the same meaning from then on. Similarly, Igor Stravinsky's ballet music *The Rite of Spring* caused a riot in Paris in 1913 and hence music has a different meaning. These are example of cultural creativity that changes the world. The same concept goes to science, engineering, sculpture, business, literature, etc., almost all realms of human activities.

We will be expecting too much of children that they show cultural creativity, although the possibility should not be ruled out totally as there are cases of very creative youngsters, but these are by definition rare. Even if it occurs, it is very rare for children to be culturally creative for the very simple reason that they do not know or have not learned enough to be creative on this scale.

Can children be creative? The answer is Yes, and No. Yes, if by creativity we mean showing personal creativity. No, if we look for cultural creativity.

If that is so, is there a place in education for personal creativity? Yes, personal creativity is the bud that may grow into cultural creativity in the long run if the conditions are right and the opportunities are there. We encourage personal creativity for two reasons. First, it is encouraging to children to be encouraged for what they can do with the knowledge and skills they have learned; it builds up their confidence. Secondly, encouraging personal creativity keeps the fire burning such that the spirit to create is sustained, with the hope that it will bloom into cultural creativity when the student has grown up and knows enough. Thus, there is a place for assessing personal creativity of school children.

How is creativity to be assessed?

We have not forgotten the bathroom scale. Just for the fun of it, you can stand on one leg on the scale to take your body weight. You can also stand on both toes to do this. Or, you may want to take your body weight squatting and stretching your arms. Whatever you do, the weight remains unchanged, practically. Standing on one leg, standing of both toes, squatting with stretched arms are possibly different styles of taking body weight. Whichever style you adopt does not change the pressure your body weight exerts on the scale, hence no change in weight. Analogically, creativity is the style a student uses his ability to do something surprising and fitting. Some children may do things more cautiously, other are more prepared to take risk. Some children use their knowledge to answer questions asking for one and only one correct answers; and, most of the questions asked in school are of this type. Other children take the question as a starting point and think in different directions. Unfortunately, those who do this are more likely to lose marks! In other words, assessment of creativity calls for a very different approach.

There is a story that a class was asked to draw a human head in an Art lesson. All children conscientiously worked on the hairs, the eyes, the nose, etc., but one. When asked, the boy replied, "I am drawing the inside of a head." The teacher said in a scolding voice, *"You don't try to be funny!"* So, the boy quickly switched to do what all other boys were doing.

Teachers need to assess creativity through judging the quality of products. Products here refer to students' works for language (e.g., from interesting short sentences to full-length stories), mathematics (e.g., new ways of solving given problems), science (e.g., useful new ways of checking on common observations), music (e.g., adding a tune to a familiar one as a *descant*), art (e.g., drawing in an unconventional way), etc. How then can the teacher assess?

Following the scheme of the famous *Torrance Test of Creative Thinking*, a product can be assessed for its creativity, or the lack of it, for four somewhat related qualities, namely, *fluency, flexibility, originality,* and *elaboration*.

Fluency: To assess fluency, just count the number of acceptable responses to a stimulus. For instance, *"Here is an empty tin-can. Think of as many ways as you can of using it."* This is an item of the *Unusual Uses Test*. Children list the uses they can think of and the teacher just counts the number of answers for a fluency score. In the school context, *"Break down the word* Singapore *and make as many other words as you can"* follows the same principle. To assess fluency, the teacher just counts the number of words students come up with. Or, *"Write as many words as you can. Each words must begin with* s *and ends with* e." For mathematics, the teacher may ask children to solve one problem in as many different ways as they can and count the number of acceptable solutions for fluency. This, of course, depends on the student's knowledge of language or mathematics as the case may be. In a sense, knowledge is the starting point of creativity.

Flexibility: This refers to the number of *categories* of responses. Take the tin-can problem. A student gives 20 different answers but the answers belong to only three categories (e.g., as container, plaything, and musical instrument). He will be awarded with a fluency score of 20 but a flexibility score of three. Here, of course, the assessment becomes somewhat subjective depending on how the teacher classifies the answers. But, then, the reliability of the scores can be counter-checked by having another teacher to classify the answers and then compare the two sets of scores given by the two teachers. It can be expected that the fluency scores are likely to be the same but the flexibility scores may differ somewhat, due to the different degrees in subjectivity involved in scoring.

Fluency and flexibility are more or less knowledge-based and you may say these are assessing learned knowledge. Yes, you are right; they do. However, research shows that children who are more fluent (knowing more) and flexible (thinking divergently) are more likely to be creative (doing many different things). After all, creativity is not something-from-nothing but something-new-from-something-old. So, knowledge does count in creativity, but it should not be static (learned for its own sake or, more likely in the school context, exam) and should go beyond (made good use of). [15]

Originality: The third quality, originality, is more attuned to what people usually talk about as creativity. Originality is the ability of coming up with *rare* answers, for example, *"Use the tin-can as a stepping stone to reach the top of a tall cupboard."* This is not a fantastic idea, but as long as only very few children give this as an answer, it is considered as being rare and therefore original. In technical sense, originality is what has been described as *statistical infrequency*. Bernard Shaw (remember the musical, *My Fair Lady*?) once said, *"The first man who describes women as flowers is a genius, the second is a fool."* Originality is also consistent with the definition that creativity as *seeing what others see but think of what others don't*. Very often, teachers will have to judge children' projects by looking at originality rather than fluency and flexibility because originality would have integrated the two more discrete qualities. This also implies that the teacher needs to be knowledgeable and experienced enough to tell the new and creative from among the old and common.

Elaboration: Finally, there is elaboration. This refers to the ability to work out the details of a creative idea. What good is it if a student has a good idea but cannot put it into practice? A student who has an interesting plot for a spy story should also be able to work out the interesting and intriguing details of the story, that is, to elaborate on the idea. The elaboration will enable others (including the teacher who is marking it) to experience the unpredictability of the twists and turns of the story.

A student who can think of three different ways of solving the same mathematic problems should be able to show the working to demonstrate his creativity, that is, to elaborate.

When Morita had the idea of Walkman, he did not work out the details himself. Elaboration was done by his engineers who had the technical competence to turn his creative idea into reality. He, however, has been credited for this invention. Thus, creative ideas and technical competence seem to be separate domains, in this case. Take an unlikely hypothetical case. Let's say you have not been trained in painting but you always have vivid images that would make interesting paintings. Let's say also that there is a technically well-trained painter who lacks imagination. What if the two of you collaborate; you provide the ideas, he paints according to what you say, and then you check whether what is painted is what you have in mind (with corrections along the way). Then, masterpieces come into existence. Who is the great artist — you or he? With the advance of technologies, such a question is not to be dismissed too lightly although it may not be found yet in the school context.

The *Creative Behaviour Scale* has items based on the above ideas of creativity. It can be used to more objectively and systematically assess a student's creativity. Needless to say, parents can use it, too.

Creative Behaviour Scale

When using the **Creative Behaviour Scale,** remember:

1. Be as objective as possible.
2. Compare the student with other students of about the same age.
3. Think of evidence that supports your rating.

Creative Behaviour Scale

Think of how he has behaved over the past three months or so. Ask whether each of the statements below describe him and how well. Use the following ratings:

4 = Very true   3 = Mostly true   2 = Often true   1 = Occasionally true

1. He is more capable and clever for a student of his age.   4 3 2 1
2. He sees things the way most other children don't.   4 3 2 1
3. He enjoys deep thinking like a little philosopher.   4 3 2 1
4. He is confident in what he does.   4 3 2 1
5. He does not depend on others to help him.   4 3 2 1
6. He prefers to do things his own way.   4 3 2 1
7. He has many interests and gets bored easily.   4 3 2 1
8. He asks a lot of questions, some sound unusual or funny.   4 3 2 1
9. He is never satisfied with simple answers.   4 3 2 1
10. He likes to solve own problem when he has one.   4 3 2 1
11. He thinks of things most other children don't.   4 3 2 1
12. He comes up with surprising ideas.   4 3 2 1
13. He does not always follow what other children do.   4 3 2 1
14. He carries on with his own ideas even if others disagree.   4 3 2 1
15. He does not give in easily to others when he disagrees.   4 3 2 1
16. He is always on the move.   4 3 2 1
17. He is rather energetic, compared with other children.   4 3 2 1
18. He moves from one activity to another and does not get tired.   4 3 2 1
19. He concentrate on his interested activities for long time.   4 3 2 1
20. He cannot be pulled away once he is engaged in his interest.   4 3 2 1
21. He works hard in what interests him.   4 3 2 1

Now that you have done the rating, it is time to draw a *Creative Behaviour Profile* for the student.

1. Find the total score for each aspect of creative behaviour according to the question numbers.
2. Circle the appropriate numbers in the right-hand block.
3. Draw lines linking one circle to the next to get the profile.
4. Find the grand total score.

Aspects	Questions	Creative Behaviour Profile									
		High				Moderate				Low	
Ability	*1–3*	12	11	10	9	8	7	6	5	4	3
Independence	*4–6*	12	11	10	9	8	7	6	5	4	3
Curiosity	*7–9*	12	11	10	9	8	7	6	5	4	3
Resourcefulness	*10–12*	12	11	10	9	8	7	6	5	4	3
Unconventionality	*13–15*	12	11	10	9	8	7	6	5	4	3
Energy	*16–18*	12	11	10	9	8	7	6	5	4	3
Conscientiousness	*19–21*	12	11	10	9	8	7	6	5	4	3

The profile you have just drawn shows where your student's strengths are and where he needs more opportunity. What about his grand total score? Where does the score place him on the scale below?

Little creative	Somewhat creative	Moderately creative	Highly creative
21–28	29–49	50–70	71–84

11. Project Work: What Is It For and How Is It Assessed?

Project work is not something coming out of the blue, it has been around for a long time. Believe it or not, it was there when I was trained as a teacher in 1954. However, in those days, project work was considered a spice to make learning more interesting occasionally. In the recent years, it has become one of the mainstay of learning. All children from kindergarten to university do project work regularly. The question: *Why project work and how is it assessed?*

The introduction of project work as a regular form of learning and assessment in Singapore schools started with the recommendation of the International Advisory Panel. The panel is mainly made up of university professors from the USA invited to study the tertiary education here many years ago. One of their recommendations is to use project grades as one of the university admission criteria.

What is project work?

Traditional learning in school is almost equated to learning from textbooks. Children are expected to understand and remember what goes between the covers of a textbook. Teachers also teach within the covers. This may be perfectly alright in the old days of schooling when learning is mainly remembering content. But now, to say that knowledge in any subject has expanded is a gross understatement. Because of this, children ought to learn not only the textbook knowledge but also knowledge beyond it and, more importantly, learn to create their own knowledge and learning how to learn. It appears that the best way to achieve this is through project work.

A project work is any learning activity which goes beyond the use of textbook as the only source of knowledge. Moreover, the new sources of knowledge need not be restricted to printed materials but may include anything from working on a model, creating a diagram, gathering numerical information (statistics), carrying out a biological experiment, etc., etc., to designing a computer programme. Yes, almost anything qualifies as a project work as long as it goes beyond reading from the textbook, although this can still be the most important learning activity.

There is another important aspect of project work; that is, working with others. In the past, a person's ability to work is assessed almost entirely on his ability to deliver what is expected of him. It did not matter much whether he got along with others. Now, the ability to work with others toward a common goal is taken seriously because many of the work today is so complicated that it takes more than one person to do it well. Therefore, team-work ability or team-spirit has become one of the criteria for being a good worker. Project work is seen therefore as the best way to develop this important personal quality of students.

Yet another important aspect of project work is that it affords the students to develop confidence and ability in presenting their ideas, especially oral presentation. A person may be good at producing whatever is produced, but the product does not always speak for itself. So, it needs a spokesman. For this reason, oral presentation skills are to be developed through project work.

Perhaps, the most important aspect of project work is that it affords the students to think and search broadly beyond the narrow scope of textbook-based knowledge, in a sense think creatively. A group of students working together on a Science project will have to do many things: to search for information from various sources (textbooks, prints and non-prints available in the school and public libraries, the Internet, CD-ROMs, resource people, etc.) They have to organize what they have read, seen, and heard and talk not only in the context of science but also the implications for the community, the society, and even the human race. They will present their knowledge in words but also through vivid and attractive images using graphics and models. If it is a History project, they will have to behave like historians trying to unveil a historical mystery. If it is a Science project, they have to behave as young scientists. In short, project work requires students to learn and, at the same time, learn how to learn.

Assessment of project work

Since project work is an all-encompassing learning experience, its assessment is also much more complicated than the assessment modes we have discussed hitherto. To begin with, the aspects of project work to be assessed needs to be specified, just like drawing up a TOS for the usual assessment.

According to the official source, four domains are to be covered in the assessment of project works. These are from the Ministry of Education's website. [16]

Domains	Learning Outcomes
Knowledge and Application	Students will acquire the ability to make links across different areas of knowledge and to generate, develop and evaluate ideas and information so as to apply these skills to the project task.
Communication	Students will acquire the skills to communicate effectively and to present ideas clearly and coherently to specific audience in both the written and oral forms.
Collaboration	Students will acquire collaborative skills through working in a team to achieve common goals.
Independent Learning	Students will be able to learn on their own, reflect on their learning and take appropriate actions to improve it.

Basically, students doing sufficient number of project works are expected to become knowledgeable, thoughtful, communicative, co-operative, and independent. These personal qualities are believed to be essential for productive and contributing citizens. The task of developing such persons is entrusted to the schools and project work is believed to be the best mechanism to achieve this goal.

As project work is open-ended, there are many possible projects on the same topics. Here lies the assessment problems. The problems are basically the same as those for assessing essays we talked about earlier: inter-rater consistency (issues of reliability) and intra-rater idiosyncrasies (issues of validity). Recall that the same answer to the vitamin question marked by 43 experienced teachers have marks differing as much as 12.5 out of 30. Recall also that such labels as *good, average,* and *weak* have different meanings given by the teachers in terms of the mark ranges. The same can well happen in the assessment of project work.

Although the data below are dated, they nevertheless illustrated well the problem of assessment of project works. [17]

1. A high-end junior college had a giant leap from having 7% distinction in one year to having 87% in the following year.
2. Another high-end junior college doubled its distinction to 85% in one year.
3. A low-end junior college had similar disparity between two years.
4. Another low-end junior college had only 7% distinction while a high-ranking one has 98%.
5. A 'neighbourhood' junior college had half of its children getting an 'A', putting it almost on par with a high-end one which had 53% 'A'.

At this juncture, as a diversion, it is interesting to look at the academic positions of the junior colleges as these have implications for the assessment and choice of topics (see later). The ranking is based on number of children with four GCE 'A'-level distinctions.

It is worthy of note that the junior colleges maintain largely their relative academic positions with slight between-year variations. In fact, the average correlation coefficient for 14 of them (excluding *Pioneer*) is a very high 0.95. It is readily appreciated that a key factor of this stability is the calibre of children posted to them. Another factor is the subject specialization since by comparison it is easier to score in Science subjects than in Arts subjects, as the content of Science subjects are relatively fixed while that of Arts subject is relatively fluid, leading to the greater probability of high scores for Science. [18]

Junior college	2000	2001	2002	2003	Median
Raffles	1	1	2	2	1.5
Hwa Chong	2	2	1	1	1.5
Victoria	4	3	3	4	3.5
National	5	4	4	3	4
Temasek	3	5	5	5	5
Anderson	6	6	6	6	6
Anglo Chinese	7	7	7	7	7
St. Andrews	8	8	8	8	8
Nanyang	9	9	10	9	9
Tampines	11	11	9	10	10.5
Pioneer	—	—	11	11	11
Jurong	10	10	13	14	11.5
Yishun	12	12	12	15	12
Catholic	13	13	14	13	13
Serangoon	14	14	15	12	14

As project work is open-ended, some degree of inconsistency is expected and should be tolerated. As students in different junior colleges had different abilities, motivation, home support, the difference between high-end and low-end junior colleges is expected within a reasonable range. However, the gross deviation is both interesting and disturbing. What could have led to this situation?

First, the topics. In the year in question, the two topics were 'Groundbreakers' and 'Entertainment'. It seemed that the first topic was more suited to the Science students whereas the second the Arts students, although with a stretch of imagination (creativity?), there can be entertaining groundbreakers and ground-breaking entertainments. Normally, students will chose a topic which is congruent to their subject specialization and teachers may have influence on the choice, too.

The topics may not be of similar (not to say, equal) difficulty in terms of concepts involved, resources available, and student interests. The different topics may also require different treatments. These do not matter if students are required to do both topics. In fact, it is better than allowing a choice, if time and markers are available. The problem of allowing choices in essay writing exams has been discussed earlier and what is mentioned there is relevant here because of the project work being open-ended.

Secondly, the teachers' roles. The dual-role of being a project adviser and then assessor gives rise to role-conflict. Normally, teachers are generous in giving guidance in project work; this is expected of them. But, when it comes to assessment, they may hesitate, quite normally, and grade conservatively lest they are seen as grade-inflating. On the other hand, they may give grades higher than the work deserves in order to encourage the students. Such a problem will not arise when marking objective tests, but project work is definitely not one of these. There may be other considerations that influence grading.

Thirdly, another aspect related to teachers is their interpretation of the topic and expectations for the submitted works. As it is always said, there are many ways to skin a cat. This is true for project work as it is for essay writing in that a topic can be interpreted variedly by teachers and students alike. When the two parties' minds do not meet, lower grades will be awarded, and vice versa. Objective tests are measuring instruments, but teacher-markers *are* the measuring instruments for supply-type assessment and, for this reason, subjectivity creeps into the scores and grades. There is no way to escape from this but to make conscious effort to minimize the disparity in marking and grading.

Just these three factors are sufficient to upset the proper grading of project work. However, there are preventive measures to pre-empt the problem. Such things as marking guidelines and training of assessors before the assessment can reduce inconsistency to some or even large extent. In fact, these are the mechanisms commonly used to ensure a higher degree of marker consistency in large-scale exams. However, to totally eliminate the subjectivity in marking open-ended products like the project work is something yet to be attainable. One has to learn to understand and accept some degree of inconsistency, at least at the systemic level, although individual children (and their parents) may feel otherwise. Ideally, an inter-rater consistency in terms of Cohen's *kappa* of 0.9 if not higher is to be aimed for; this high expectation is because the marks and grades are going to impact on the students as *individuals,* affecting their future development and opportunity for development. This seems somewhat demanding, but then the grades are used to make critical decisions on the individuals and not as a group for research purpose. This is analogous to the requirement of score reliability of 0.9 and above for standardized tests the results of which are used to make important and irrevocable decision on individuals.

Let's take a diversion and go back to the bathroom scale analogy. You wish to weigh your body, and you go to buy a scale. In the shop, you are shown many models which differ in size and shape and colour. You are also told that these have not been calibrated or standardized such that the same object weighted on the different scales will have different weights. Which one do you take? Teacher-markers marking open-ended products such as essays and projects are like the un-calibrated scales, each one has her own way of assessing the same work (as shown by the vitamins question earlier). They can be useful only if they can be calibrated to give highly similar results to the same piece of student work.

Besides the preventive measures, there is the *post hoc* moderation. Moderation is the adjustment of exam results to fit into an expected distribution. It is a 'closing the gate after the sheep is gone' approach and is a common practice in large-scale exams. For project work, this is first done at the junior college level to iron out discrepancy among teachers within the same college. Then there is the national level moderation which aims to maintain a common 'standard' across junior colleges. Here, again, perfection is unattainable and some degree of discrepancy is to be expected and, more importantly, accepted or, in fact, tolerated.

The above discussion uses the historical case of pre-university project work to illustrate problems inherent in it as a method of assessment, because of its open-ended nature. The points made are relevant to project work at the levels of secondary and primary schools, and even kindergarten.

What else can be considered?

Project work as a teaching device is useful to broaden the scope of learning, both in terms of knowledge acquisition and the development of study habits, skills, and attitudes. In this sense, it affords the students with the opportunity to experience a more balanced kind of learning as compared with learning from textbooks alone. If project work is done just for these benefits without assessment, those problem discussed above will not arise. But, then, in a system where assessment plays a critical role, non-exam learning is likely to be neglected such that what needs to be developed is not given a chance. So, assessment of project work at all levels is to stay. A relevant question is what can be considered and tried to minimize the ills of assessing such open-ended products.

When students are doing project work, what can and should teachers do? First of all, project work is interesting and students may become so interested that they get too involved or even taken over. Refrain from this.

Next, and teachers can help in pointing to available resources and make them available when necessary. Let the student learn to sort out problems and make good use of the resources; let them become independent learners. Then, if it is a group project, see that the students co-ordinate and co-operate and make good use of their individual strengths to contribute to the group's common goal. In short, teachers should behave like a good coach and not a player. Remember, what you do to help students doing project work affects the validity of its assessment.

Of course, parents are interested in the grades the projects get in the end. This is where the assessment comes in.

A single total score is most convenient for making administrative decision such as pass-fail or selection-rejection. It is mainly for this reason that a grade is awarded for a project work. And, the problem is that we are so used to the single score or grade so much so that we close our eyes to alternatives.

The purpose of introducing project work into the curriculum is to develop a few discrete strengths in the children beyond knowledge acquisition. Even just for knowledge, we hope the children learn more broadly and are able to integrate knowledge of different strands. Beyond knowledge, there are the ability to communicate orally and in written form, the ability to work with others and contribute to common goal, the ability to solve problem by themselves, and to stand up for their own views. Admittedly, strength in one of these may interact with the rest to some extent, but they are of different nature and need to be seen and assessed as such.

This being the case, it is obvious that knowledge, communication, collaboration, and independence *do not add up*. Of course, arithmetically, scores for the four aspects of a project work can always be summed to form a total score. The question is what such a total score means. Moreover, different students getting the same total score (or overall grade) are not likely to be the same kind of persons; they have many different routes (combinations of scores) to the same total. Furthermore, and more fundamentally, adding scores of the discrete strengths implies that weakness in one can be compensated by strength in another — a very knowledgeable but non-communicative student is as good as his peer who lacks knowledge but is impressively communicative. Perhaps, we should learn to be more comfortable with profiles although this may be more time-consuming and administratively clumsy to use for making decisions.

Reconciling assessment disparity

If it is necessary to use a single score or grade for the assessment of project work in the reality of school, some ways can be tried to reconcile marker-inconsistency. These may include product-sample scale, scaling, and project proposal.

Product-sample scale: This technique can be used at the school and systemic levels. First take a random sample of between 12 and 24 projects and have them independently assessed by two or more experienced markers. The sampled projects are to be distributed into six (or any other number of categories desired, say, nine) piles in terms of overall merit. Then, compare the two markers' grading and sort out any gross discrepancy (i.e., more than one grade difference). Cohen's *kappa* can then be calculated for an objective evaluation of the inter-rater consistency of the grades awarded by the pair of markers. As an alternative, Fleiss's *kappa* can be calculated for more than two markers at one go. Then, aim for a *kappa* of 0.7 or greater for a satisfactory inter-rater agreement. When sorted out, the six piles serve as an anchorage. Once this product-sample scale of marked projects is completed, it serves as a yardstick or common reference for further assessment. The remaining projects will then be matched with the sampled projects for overall quality and given the corresponding grades. [19, 20]

Scaling: This is a *post hoc* solution to the problem of marker-inconsistency. After the projects have been assessed by different markers, a sample of between eight and 12 is taken from each of the marker and the grades they awarded are aligned. Then, look into the qualitative aspects of the projects in each grade to see if they are similar in quality. For instance, a project obtains a B from one marker but a similar one a C from another marker. Then, it is necessary to come to an agreement that whether it deserves a B or C. Do this for all the other grades. Once done, all grades given earlier will have to be adjusted according to the agreed standard. In a sense, this is the reverse of product-sample scale. The purpose is to ensure projects of similar quality are awarded the same grade. Admittedly, this is much more tedious and time-consuming than the earlier method.

Project proposal: This is yet to be first convinced and then tried. This is more suitable for higher class level, say, secondary and above. Since students have been doing project work starting at the primary level, they would have completed 10 or more projects when they reach secondary school. The experience would have built up their relevant skills and attitudes to a large extent, albeit at a lower level. To assess their ability in *planning* project work, they can be given a number of suitable topics and asked to write project proposals for these, *without actually carrying out the projects*. They will then be assessed on the qualities of the project proposals for clarity of project objectives, scope and suitability of resources, appropriateness of information organization, effectiveness of written (or oral) presentation, etc., etc. In short, this is an assessment of *process* — an assessment of how well the students can plan projects cohesively and systematically and their resourcefulness.

Without actually carrying out the projects? Yes, because the focus and interest is whether the students can plan (including foreseeing problems of implementation). After all, architects must be good in planning and not laying the bricks, and electrical engineers must be good in designing circuits and not wiring them. Of course, a balance between planning (theoretical work) and hands-on (practical work) is desirable and this can be built into the instruction. By the way, it is interesting to note that in quite a number of American universities, Master's degree students are expected to submit and defense workable research proposals without dirtying their hands with actual data. The assumption seems to be that if they are able to plan research well, they will be able to actualize it when necessary. Besides, when they become full-fledged researchers, their research assistants will do the leg work, leaving them to do the brain work (thinking). It is for this that an eminent researcher says that a real researcher does the beginning (planning) and the end (interpreting) and leaves others to do what goes in-between.

One possible drawback of this approach to the assessment of project work is that what is not assessed is not taught. Teachers may spend more or all time training their students in writing project proposals. Another ill-effect of this is that it deprives the students of the opportunity and joy of doing projects. This, of course, need to be monitored and, when necessary, controlled. And, a good balance between theory and practice is needed.

Concluding remarks

Like any other kind of learning, project work can be exciting or discouraging, depending on how it is done. Whatever it is to the individual students and teachers, consistent assessment is a problem due to its open-endedness. Ways and means have been tried to cope with this critical aspect and new ways and means need to be sought and tried. The ultimate aim is to educate the students more broadly without getting them confused by the grades they are given at the end of doing a project.

12. Rubrics and *Assessment for Learning*

When Samuel takes his oral exam, he gets 15 of the possible 20 marks. His father intuitively converts that into 75 percent and thinks "that's not bad, three-quarter way to perfection," but his mother thinks "that's not good enough, still one-quarter away from the perfect mark." Beyond these, Samuel and his parents know nothing more about the boy's performance.

This seems to be a very common reaction of children and their parents to marks and grades. They care so much more about marks and so much less about the performance. They are not to blame as marks seem to be the only information the school provides them with. A mark symbolizes a performance level to children, parents, teachers, and school leaders. It is supposed to be the be all and end all of learning. This is the traditional approach of *assessment **of** learning.*

American and British educationists have, in the recent years, been calling for more attention to be paid to *assessment for learning.* Some even goes to the extent to suggest that formal big-bang exams be abolished. Reasons put up in support of this include educational ills such as teaching-to-the-test, curtailment of curriculum, exam stress, grade inflation, etc., etc., and even *cheating* by schools. To some extent, these are true, but the debate goes on.

As whatever happens in American and British education scene is highly likely to appear here some years later, so is the advocacy for *assessment for learning.*

Why *assessment for learning?*

As in Samuel's case, the mark shows how well he has done in the oral exam, but it does not tell anything beyond it. The boy and his parents have no way to know what he has done and specifically what and how he can do better next round. Since 15 out of 20 is three-quarter and 75 percent, that's all they are given to know.

To be fair, the teacher-examiners would have used some kind of guidelines when assessing, but this information are not available to the students and their parents. In some other assessment situations, there may not be guidelines, and teachers rely on their personal experience and expectation; assessment thus becomes highly subjective and vague.

For effective learning, along the way, there is a need for timely and specific feedback which tells the students where they have done well and where they need to put in more efforts. Moreover, such information cannot be packaged just as a number. Analogously, we need to see where we are heading to when we are driving, along the way and not only when the car stops; by then, it may be too late.

The need for timely and specific feedback during learning gives rise to the increasing popularity of *assessment rubrics* (or just *rubrics*). In contrast to *assessment of learning*, rubrics are meant to be effective tools for *assessment for learning*. **For** instead of **of** because the information gathered through rubrics is to indicate along the way the effectiveness and directions of learning and not the end-product of learning. Such information is to *guide* learning rather than to *judge* learning. In the assessment jargon, using rubrics for assessment *for* learning is *formative* whereas giving a total mark at the end of learning is *summative*.

Research has shown that marks at the end of a long journey of learning do not help students learn better; they come too late to be useful. Even written comments by teachers (say, on essays) are ignored. However, feedback and discussion using assessment rubrics have produced better effects in secondary students' learning in a British experiment in some secondary schools in London. The magic seems to lie with the timely and specific information on the progress of learning which helps to develop the students' sense of responsibility for their own learning.

What is an assessment rubric?

A rubric is, according to the *New Webster's Dictionary of English Language*, originally, "*the directions and rule for the conduct of a service, often printed in red; an ecclesiastical or Episcopal rule or injunction."* Thus, it is another instance that there is nothing new under the sun, although assessment rubrics have gained popularity among Singapore schools only recently, perhaps, in a different context.

How then does a rubric look like? For this, we need to return to the rating scale. In fact, rubrics are nothing more than detailed rating scales given a modern look but using an age-old name. Take oral presentation of project work as an example. In the old days, a rating scale for assessing oral presentation may look so simple like this:

Oral presentation	Poor	Acceptable	Good	Excellent
	1	2	3	4

From this, the teacher will give a grade according to her judgment where *1* represents a poor performance and *4* an excellent one. How the teacher comes to the conclusion only she knows. Getting a *3* (Good) does not tell the student (and the school leaders and parents) anything more than that the teacher is impressed. However, common sense tells us that there are aspects of oral presentation which can and should be assessed separately. So, the simple one-criterion rating scale is now elaborated in terms of several criteria to be covered, thus:

	Poor	Acceptable	Good	Excellent
Organization	1	2	3	4
Subject knowledge	1	2	3	4
Graphics	1	2	3	4
Mechanics	1	2	3	4
Eye contact	1	2	3	4
Elocution	1	2	3	4

Now, the six aspects covered in the assessment are specified and each is graded on four levels. This shows that the same assessment procedure is repeated once for each of the six sub-skills of oral presentation. With more information given, the student and parents know more about where the boy's strengths and weakness are. A student who organizes the presentation very well gets a *4* for organization, but he may get a *1* for eye contact because he does not look at his audience at all, that is, not engaging them. Different students get different profiles as they have different strengths and weaknesses. Thus, the profile tells more about a presentation than just a global score does.

With a rubric like that, it is possible that different students get the same total score but have different strengths and weaknesses. The total scores are the same, but they are strong or weak in different aspects and therefore have different learning needs. This is where rubrics are most useful, proving specific information of individual students.

Then, another problem arises. What does it mean to be *poor, acceptable, good*, or *excellent* in, say, organization — just one of the six sub-skills? To make the meaning of each grade clearer, the quality is spelt out in terms of student behaviour. With this elaboration, the scales now look like this (just the first two aspects to illustrate). [21]

	Poor 1	**Acceptable 2**	**Good 3**	**Excellent 4**
Organization	Audience cannot understand presentation because there is no sequence of information.	Audience has difficulty following presentation because student jumps around.	Student presents information in logical sequence which audience can follow.	Student presents information in logical, interesting sequence which audience can follow.
Graphics	Student uses superfluous graphics or no graphics	Student occasionally uses graphics that rarely support text and presentation.	Student's graphics relate to text and presentation.	Student's graphics explain and reinforce screen text and presentation.

Now, a good organization is characterized as *Student presents information in logical sequence which audience can follow*. And, excellence in graphics means *Student's graphics explain and reinforce screen text and presentation*. It is obvious that such descriptions are more informative than a mere *good* or *excellent* and definitely much more than a single score for the oral presentation as a whole.

Such assessment not only passes judgments but also give directions, hence *assessment for learning*. It forces the teacher to be specific rather than vague when assessing. And, the use of rubrics enhances the assessment with better communication between teachers and children (and their parents). Moreover, when teachers design their own rubrics, they have to be analytical and thorough for those sub-skills they will assess, and this thinking process sharpens their minds so that they become more discerning.

However, in spite of the specificity, the descriptive statements are still open to interpretation to some extent, though. For example, the description for excellent organization has the adjective *interesting*. But, what is interesting to one teacher may not be so to another, and the same student performance may get a *4* from one teacher but a *3* from the other. After all, words are words. This, however, underlines the importance of careful choice of words when designing a rubric.

However, rubrics represent clearly an improvement over global rating scales as contrasted in the table below.

	Rating scale	**Rubrics**
Clarity	Numbers to indicate the degree of merit, but meaning can be vague.	Statements are used to describe quality of performance.
Validity	Raters are likely to focus on different aspects of a performance.	Raters focus of the same specified aspects of a performance.
Reliability	Inter-rater agreement is always doubtful.	Scale points are defined in terms of expected qualities or behaviors.

Use of rubrics

The example given above is for the assessment of oral presentation. However, rubrics are versatile assessment tools and can be used for many other kinds of performance and products so far as the qualities of performance and products can be specified. Instances include singing a song, drawing a picture, acting a character, constructing a model, reciting a poem, giving an impromptu speech, participating in a group discussion, etc., etc. Almost anything that can be seen or heard can be assessed with the use of rubrics. In other words, rubrics can be used in conjunction with some forms of *authentic learning* — learning that requires children to perform, act, or produce.

Advocates of rubrics also suggest that students be involved in the design of rubrics. In other words, students are not only to be assessed passively by teachers' rubrics but to develop rubrics that will be used to assess their own learning. It is believed that, in so doing, students will be sensitized to their learning needs, see the directions they can take, set learning goals for themselves, and feel an ownership of their own learning.

Nevertheless, one advantage of this is sure. When students are assessed by teacher-developed rubrics and given a copy after assessment, they may not really understand the descriptive statements. The concepts may not be understood. The wording may be too difficult. Such conditions nullify the purpose of feedback. On the other hand, when students are guided to design their own rubrics, teachers can make sure that the students understand the concepts and wording. In this sense, they know what will be assessed and how such understanding will give learning a clear direction. Moreover, the process of designing their own rubrics means the students are previewing the learning — just like reading up on a country you are going to visit and this gives more meaning to the trip.

Of course, a prerequisite of this is that the students are mature enough to understand those concepts involved and are proficient in language used to describe the qualities of learning. Likewise, when the parents receive the rubrics assessing and reporting on their children's learning, they need to be familiar with the concepts listed therein and understand the statements or descriptions, that is to say, these ought to mean the same things to the parents as they are to the teachers. In a very real sense, when teachers learn to develop and use rubrics to assess student learning, parents also need to learn and understand the information contained in a set of rubrics, if they are to help their students in learning and be partners to the school and teachers in the students' learning journey.

Rubric scores

This is a controversy. As pointed out earlier, parents are used to total score as indicators of performance. Parents are naturally influenced by this practice. In spite of the fact that the purpose of using rubrics is to gain detailed information about learning and to use such information to guide further learning, we still look for a total score. Perhaps because of this deeply ingrained tradition, some rubrics provide for total scores which usually are simple sums of the scores for the different aspects (sub-skills) covered in a rubric.

The fictitious cases below show clearly the problem of using total scores of rubrics. Since the three boys all get 15 as the total scores, in terms of *assessment of learning*, they are considered as being equally competent. But, from the perspective of *assessment for learning*, they obviously need different guidance. Albert needs to improve on graphics and mechanics, Alfred organization and subject knowledge, and Andrew graphics and eye contact. They are obviously not equals and not the same kind of students.

	Albert	Alfred	Andrew
Organization	4	*1*	2
Subject knowledge	4	*1*	3
Graphics	*1*	4	*1*
Mechanics	*1*	4	4
Eye contact	3	3	*1*
Elocution	2	2	4
Total	15	15	15

In short, the same total scores can be obtained from very different profiles and the use of total scores masks the subtle yet important differences. This in a very real sense is self-defeating and self-contradictory. This problem arises partly because of the old habit of using total scores and partly is due to confusion between *formative* and *summative* assessment.

This last point deserves some elaboration. If the two approaches to assessment are not kept clearly apart, what might happen? For instance, adding up total scores for a series of rubrics used for *assessment for learning* over a period of time and treating the totals as a summative measure for *assessment of learning*, then, there is no need for big-bang exams which cause exam stress (especially to the students and parents). This is also administratively convenient since the scores can be stored in the computer for subsequent processing. In short, this is killing two birds with one stone.

The problem is when a series of rubric scores are known to the students and their parents to be used for summative purposes, *assessment for learning* takes on the role of *assessment of learning*, and a series of formative assessment is turned literally into a series of mini-summative assessment. The end result is the multiplication of exam stress and the function of rubrics as a guide to effective learning may be lost. To reiterate, it is important that the two forms of assessment, *formative* and *summative*, are kept distinctively separate.

Reliability and validity of rubric assessment

Being an assessment tool, rubrics need to show that the scores or grades obtained through using them are consistent (reliable) and valid (truly reflecting what is assessed). Without these, the scores and grades cannot be trusted, just as it is for scores obtained through the use of other forms of assessment.

To check grading consistency, two teachers independently assess a group of students on their performance. The grades are then entered into the Cohen's *kappa* calculator (e.g., http://vassarstats.net/kappa.html). As shown in the example below, the two teachers are consistent in grading 17 of the 20 students (3 AA, 5 BB, 5 CC, and 4 DD) but inconsistent in three cases (1 AB, 1 BC, and 1DC). This gives a Cohen's *kappa* of 0.80 which is considered as very good, that is, can be largely trusted though not perfectly.

Teacher A	Teacher B				
	A	B	C	D	Row total
A	3	1			4
B		5	1		6
C			5		5
D			1	4	5
Column total	3	6	7	4	20

As for checking validity, there are basically two approaches: checking internal consistency of sub-skills and checking against external criteria. These are done through finding the correlations of one kind or another.

First, the internal check. It makes sense that when a rubric has several sub-skills (aspects), they tend to be related such that children good in one tend to be good also in another. For instance, children who are more knowledgeable in a subject tend to be more able to organize the knowledge. In statistical sense, organization and knowledge tends to be positively correlated. And, if it is indeed indicated by the obtained correlation coefficient, this is an evidence of grade or score validity of the rubric (or at least part of it). However, it is necessary to watch out for possible Halo Effect. This happens when a good rating on an earlier assessed aspect influences subsequent assessment of other aspects.

Next is the external check. It stands to reason that students who get higher grading for organization or knowledge will also get higher marks for a separate relevant test of subject knowledge. Thus, the correlation between rubric grades and external test scores can be calculated. If the correlation coefficient is of a reasonable magnitude, it is taken as evidence of validity. Alternatively, students can be first grouped as high or low in rubric grades and then compared on their respective group means for the scores of a knowledge test.

In short, rubric scores or grades are not self-evident of their reliability and validity. Such evidence needs be procured for them to be trusted. Not to do so amounts to blind faith, ignorance, or sheer laziness, or all.

Concluding remarks

Going back to the example this chapter begins with, had Samuel come home with not only a mark of 15 for his oral exam but also a copy of rubrics on which some descriptive statements have been circled to indicate his strengths, he and his parents would be in a better position to see what to improve on. The reason for using rubrics is to gain a deeper understanding and a more complete picture of what has and has not taken place in learning. The information is reflective of learning as an on-going process and not as an end-state. Thus, it is well-advised, again, to keep apart summative *assessment **of** learning* and formative *assessment **for** learning*.

13. Above-level Testing: Good or Bad?

One day, Samuel came home and told me that only 5 percent of his class passed the Literature exam because the teacher used the Secondary 4 standard to mark the Secondary 2 students' papers. On an earlier occasion, he grumbled that only 25 percent of his cohort passed the Math exam, again, because the teachers used a Secondary 4 paper. I thought such above-level assessment is peculiar to his school, one of the 10 Special Assistance Plan Schools. Being curious about how common this practice is among other schools, I told the story to a group of teachers attending my action research workshop and the response was an astonishingly resounding "We all do that!"

Obviously, above-level testing seems to be quite common among schools in Singapore. But, why?

Out-of-level testing (OLT) in the United States

OLT may take two forms: below-level testing and above-level testing. These have been done in the United States for specific purposes with specific assumptions.

In America, OLT has a long history and refers to administering tests of a lower level to children, for instance testing Grade 5 children with Grade 4 exam. This form of OLT usually involves children who are weak at a class level. It is also called *off-grade* testing or *instructional level* testing. In 1993, only one state allowed this form of OLT. The number has since increased to six states in 1995 and 10 in 1997. Common reasons given for below-level testing are: (1) it reduces student frustration and emotional trauma; (2) it improves accuracy of measurement; and (3) it better matches the student's current educational goals and instructional level. However, such arguments have their supporters but also invited rebuttals. [22]

Opposite to below-level testing is the above-level testing where children take tests of higher standards than their current grades, for example, Third Grade children taking the Fifth Grade exam. Such testing is carried out to identify gifted and talented children who are achieving at the top end (e.g. 95th percentile), far above their current grade level. There are advocates who support such testing and there are detractors who disagree.

Above-level testing in Singapore

The experience of the Secondary 2 students cited above is more like the second kind of OLT — above-level testing. It is not known exactly how common above-level OLT is in Singapore schools. An accurate picture of the situation requires a proper survey but if above-level testing turns out to be a widely common practice among Singapore schools of all levels, it does not come as a surprise in a highly competitive context.

The teachers, in doing above-level testing, perhaps, hope to achieve better assessment results by challenging the children with a higher standard to motivate them to study harder. Motivating student learning is indeed one of the several functions of assessment although it is not, need not, and should not be the most important function. With above-level testing, children are more likely to do poorly, scoring lower marks than they deserve, and this is likely to lead to parents pressurizing children to learn harder, leading to indirectly motivating the children through their parents.

However, a difference needs to be made between above-level testing for identifying academically excellent students as is done in USA and motivating and challenging students here in Singapore. Questions can be raised: Does such testing really motivate and challenge students? Which group of students will be positively influenced by such testing? What other consequences may result, in the short run? And, in the long haul?

Assumed benefits

There are several possible benefits for above-level testing. Cognitively, taking an above-level test gives the children a chance to experience in a concrete manner the demands of the more difficult tasks. This feeding-forward may orientate the students to future challenges and set a clearer focus for their learning. It may work for conscientious and high-achieving children, perhaps those in the top quartile (i.e., 25 percent) of a class. It may not work for children in general, especially the unmotivated (and always non-achieving) ones to whom schooling serves purposes other than learning.

Emotionally, the more challenging tasks may motivate and force some children to study harder, especially if they fail to cope with the above-level tasks. Some high-ability children take occasional failures as challenges with the belief that failure is the mother of success. They will work harder to maintain their self-image of being capable. Children's difficulty in coping with above-level testing may give teachers and parents good reasons to press the children to study even harder. Such social motivation is legitimized over and above the self-motivation some capable children may already have. This double dose of internal and external motivation will impact the conscientious and achieving children to maintain a high level of effort.

Undesirable consequences

The assumed benefits above are what they are — *assumed*. They may and may not materialize, depending on other factors. These are explicated below.

Unfamiliar content and untaught skills: First of all, above-level tests contain items, testing materials and skills which the children are not familiar with or have not been taught. These built-in characteristics prevent the students from doing well as they should for level-appropriate tests. Thus, excellent children may turn out to be mislabeled as mediocre. The above-level testing results do not truthfully reflect the capability of high-ability children in the proper context of their current grades; measurement-wise, the above-level testing results are not valid.

Low score reliability: Secondly, as is true of all level-appropriate tests, there are more items and questions in the middle range (i.e., moderate F's between 0.4 and 0.6) of the ability tested and fewer at the two extremes (i.e., high and low F's). As a result, score reliability is higher for scores in the middle of the score distribution and lower for scores away from the centre of score distribution. When above-level testing is conducted, children are likely to obtain low to mediocre scores, and this means much of the scores are less reliable. Thus, above-level testing results are less trustworthy as a measure of student ability. However, when repeatedly tested, the students are likely to get lower marks than they deserve. This, measurement-wise, leads to a paradoxically high reliability — students are doing poorly again and again.

Beyond zone of proximal development: It is a well-known fact that children learn more effectively when the learning tasks are within the *zone of proximal development* (ZPD). The concept of ZDP originated from the Russian psychologist Lev Vygotsky and is defined as the distance between the actual developmental level as determined by independent problem solving and the level of potential development as determined through problem solving under adult guidance, or in collaboration with more capable peers. In view of this, children who sit for the above-level testing may feel that they have been thrown into the deep end of the pool. They sink most of the time and occasionally swim. Another analogy is that the students are doing high-jumping when the bar is raised too high beyond their current ability level.

Frustration and its correlates: If above-level testing fails three-quarters or more of the students, it deserves serious consideration for its probable negative effects on them. Occasional frustration is a normal experience in life and its ill-effect may soon dissipate in most cases. However, constant frustration resulting from repeated above-level testing has adverse psychological and social effects, and may possibly lead to some long-lasting undesirable consequences.

At the personal level, repeated failure to cope with above-level tests creates in the individual children a wrong image of *being unable*. There are sufficient research studies on learned helplessness of animals and human learners to show that constant failure leads to unwillingness to try (de-motivated) as it has an incapacitating effect. Research also shows that this is difficult to eradicate even when the negative condition has changed to be positive.

A related phenomenon is the development of *externality* (in contrast of *internality*) as a consequence of repeated and constant failure. Children who keep failing tend to attribute their failure to external factors such as bad luck, favouritism, or the 'powerful others'. They thus develop an *external locus of control* and lack faith in their own ability to influence events around them. Conversely, successful children develop a sense of self-worth, self-confidence, or internal locus of control, believing in their own ability to control their destiny.

At the societal level, a natural reaction to failing an above-level test is the feeling of injustice. When such a test is administered, children who could not cope feel that the teacher has not been fair since many of the materials or skills are not familiar as they have not been taught. Parents who come to know about this are likely to experience the same feeling of injustice that their children are tested beyond what they have been taught.

When done over a long period of time, the sense of injustice accumulates and it may be seen as an inherent quality of the education system and even the society. In the long run, students' (and their parents') sense of injustice, created by conditions beyond their control, will be transferred to the system and society and this actually goes against the grain of democracy and fairness.

When above-level testing is practised often and widely, it will create generations of future citizens who lack confidence as they have been regularly made to feel frustrated and incapable.

False information

Testing is the way to get information about student learning. The information is first and foremost used to inform children how well they have learned and what more they need to do. For these purpose, the information in terms of scores must be reliable and valid. This leads to the question of how reliable and valid scores for above-level testing are.

First, reliability. Scores for above-level testing are highly reliable, for the simple reason that the test is beyond the children' ability and they most likely will fail and fail if taking the same test twice or many times. It is just like whatever a perpetual liar says; he is highly reliable, consistently saying things that are not true.

Next, validity. This is the real problem with above-level testing.

In the figure below, the taller curve at the centre shows the distribution of scores for a test which is appropriate to the children in term of their ability. The average performance centres around the score 1.0, and the mode (i.e., most popular score), the median (i.e., a score that separate the children into two-halves, or the middle-most score), and the mean (i.e., average of all scores) are very close to one another. This is expected when a set of scores yielded approximately a normal distribution. The slight differences among the mode, the median, and the mean indicate that the test is only slightly above-level, but these can be 'ignored' as due to measurement error (i.e., fluctuation caused by sampling).

The lower curve, with a long tail toward the high end, is the result of an above-level testing. On this curve, there are much more low scores and much fewer high scores, since the test is a difficult one far above the head of the students. (Incidentally, this will be a good test for, say, scholarship selection.) Next, the mean is located at 0.4, instead of 1.0, since it is an above-level test.

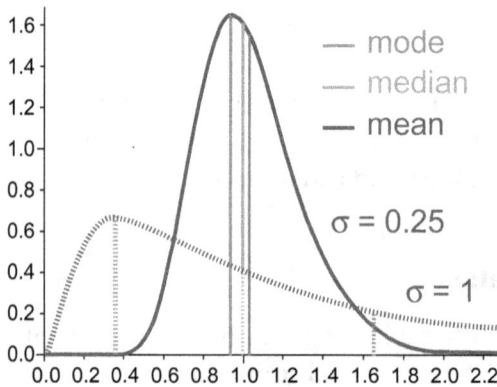

These mean many students are getting lower scores than they deserve and the scores under-estimated the actual individual abilities, perhaps with the exception of a few very high-scoring ones who are lucky enough to escape the assault. How the students thus treated will react emotionally has been alluded to above. For the parents, they get the wrong information that the children are weak when this is not true. They may be aware that an above-level test was used (perhaps, intentionally) and therefore do not worry too much, but the information they get is still a false information which does not reflect the true situation.

In short, above-level testing yields false information about the children and such information mislead children and their parents. Moreover, intentionally producing false information is tantamount to forgery.

The way ahead

Above-level testing must have been introduced by a school or a few in the beginning with a specific purpose. The assumed benefits discussed earlier may or may not have been realized or actualized, but the probabilities of undesirable consequences would have happened. To avoid further aggravation and to protect the children from unnecessary psychological stress or trauma, some cautions are suggested below.

Context: To benefit children with above-level testing, the context needs to be made clear to them. Doing so will reduce much of the anxiety before testing and frustration after testing. It may also avoid misunderstanding. Children need to be clearly told that it is done to familiarize them with the requirement and standards of the above-level tests. In short, it is done as a *mock* or rehearsal assessment and the marks should not be counted in their achievement records.

Frequency and timing: Since above-level testing is done as mock or rehearsal assessment, it needs be done intermittently (perhaps, once a semester or even just half-yearly) with advanced notice. Forewarned means fore-armed; students should not be caught by surprise. They should be psychologically prepared to take above-level testing. This may be done best after normal assessment towards the end of each semester (or half year) after the formal exams so that there is a clear distinction between the real assessment and the mock assessment.

Participation: As above-level testing is potentially stressful and even traumatic, care needs to be exercised to involve only children proven to be in the top end of performance overall or in specific subjects; this could mean those in the top 15–25 percent of a cohort and who have consistently done well in their studies. Moreover, participation is best if it is voluntary, to avoid children feeling being pressurized into it.

Debriefing: Many students will find the above-level testing much more difficult than their normal assessment. To eliminate the painful stress of not being able to cope, proper debriefing after the assessment needs be conducted to help the students, especially those who have failed, to see the results in the right perspective. Moreover, a thorough discussion on the materials and skills (which they are yet to acquire) will motivate and orientate the children to achieve success.

Ethics: Whether a student passes or fails the above-level tests, the scores do not validly indicate their true ability levels. This raises an ethical concern: Should the students be given false information about their achievement and ability, as it definitely has a negative impact on them?

Conclusion

Above-level testing is assumed to be beneficial but its real benefits need to be objectively evaluated. The intention may be good, but the probable undesirable consequences are not to be overlooked. Even more fundament is its logic, as some Secondary Three students who were above-level tested rightly reflected, *"If we can pass the tests, then the school should promote us to Sec Four."*

The Chinese parable below is relevant to above-level testing.

Once upon a time, an old farmer planted a plot of rice. He saw the young shoots break through the soil and grow taller each day. Impatient by nature, he was not satisfied with their slow growth rate.

At night, he asked himself, "How can I get the plants to grow faster?" Suddenly, he jumped out of bed and dashed to the field. Under the moonlight, he began pulling up the young shoots by half an inch. Pleased with his work, he said to himself, "What a great idea! Look, how much taller the plants are now!" Satisfied, he went back home.

The next morning he told his son proudly about what he had done. His son was awed and ran to the field only to find all the young plants dying.

Note: An earlier version of this chapter appears in *i.d.e.a²*, *Issue 2*, of the Academy of Singapore Teachers, October 2011.

14. Grade Point Average: Beware of Its Pitfalls

Grade point average (GPA) is commonly used in universities and polytechnics all over the world. It is not so popular with secondary schools and even less so with primary schools, where total score (aggregate) is used to indicate a student's general or overall performance; there are of course exceptions. Nevertheless, since the majority of secondary school students ultimately go to a university or polytechnic, it is good for school leaders, teachers, and parents to know about GPA.

How is GPA calculated?

Depending on the assessment policies of the individual institutions of learning, the actual calculation of GPA varies. However, generally, the procedure is conceptually this:

$$GPA = \text{Sum of Credits} * \text{Points} / \text{Total credits}$$

Here, Credits are the "weights" of courses, with courses presumably more important carrying more credits. Points are the marks corresponding to a grade earned; for example, in the American system, a grade of A+ or A is given 4.0 points, B+ 3.3, C+ 2.3, etc. Thus, the points reflect the performance as assessed by the course tutor. Therefore, Credit*Points indicates how well a student has done in a course of certain importance. When the student have completed several courses, he has earned several Credits*Points. Then, these are summed and then divided by the total number of Credits, the result is his GPA, which indicates his overall performance in the programme he studies.

This sounds simple and straightforward but it may not be really so. Many institutions have grades not only for the various courses but also marks for them. And, then, there is a scheme showing the mark ranges for each grade. For example, in the American system, A+ has a mark range 80–100, B+ 70–79, etc.

As will be shown later, when a grade is awarded for a course as test, exam, or project result, there is no problem. The problem comes when the grades for different courses are converted to points and then the aggregated points are averaged to arrive at the GPA. Moreover, the mark ranges vary from countries to countries and this is a problem of comparability which may advantage or disadvantage students depending on which country they come from.

How did GPA come about?

There is an interesting history of GPA, which you may not want to believe.

The story dated back to the 18th Century and the place was Cambridge, one of England's two academic strongholds. William Farish (1759–1837) was a Chemistry and Natural Philosophy tutor at the University, who was well-known for the development of isometric projection and attributed the invention of the first university examination system. The two things Farish was good at have something in common, "metric". For this, he could have been seen as an expert in measurement and whatever he did and said about measurement would carry weight, especially when he was among the dons of a university no less than Cambridge. After all, if Farish was able to handle complex measurement problem in Chemistry, measurement in education should not be a problem to him, or should it be?

Being a junior staff (since he was not a professor but a tutor), Farish might have had a more than usual heavy load of marking. Moreover, in those days when "payment by pieces" could well be the mode of employment, he needed to mark as many essays as he could manage. As we know, marking essays analytically is very time-consuming and very brain-taxing. So, Farish needed to find a way to cope with these problems.

One of those busy days after exams, he passed by a cobbler's shop. He stood there and watched how the cobbler works, perhaps, just to relieve himself from the tiresome marking. Then, he noticed that the cobbler classified the completed shoes into piles according to his judgement of the quality and gave them grades such as A, B, C, etc. This gave Farish an idea: why not sort out the essays into piles of different qualities as he saw them and assign grades? So, the essay grading system was born! It definitely is a surprise that Farish, being an academic, borrowed this idea from the shoe industry where workers were paid by the number of shoes (Hartman, Jaksa, & Pallandino, 2000), but it serves a useful purpose. Somehow, words went around that a new and efficient method of assessing a large number of essays was invented and used in Cambridge. If it was good enough for Cambridge, it should be more than good enough for lesser universities. And, so, Farish's grading system became popular in England and later America, naturally, and then the world. And, in present day measurement terminology, there is a special terms for it, *global, holistic, or impressionistic marking*, which has its strengths and weakness only to be found out later by researchers. Note that, up to this point, Farish's system deals only with grading and does not involve averaging.

What then are problems with GPA?

When Farish's grading system is used to assess a set of objects (say, essays) on their relative merits (however defined), it causes no problem, as long as we remember the grades are (1) relative and not absolute (i.e., A is better than B which is better than C and so on) and (2) poorly defined (i.e., we cannot really tell how much is A better than B and so on). This serves the purpose of telling which students have done better than others, in the eye of the tutor.

The problem arises when numeric grades (1, 2, 3, etc.) are used in place of letter grades (A, B, C, etc.). When letter grades are used, we know very well that we cannot add two letters to arrive at a third, not to say, averaging them. If A = 1, B = 2, C = 3, D = 4, E = 5, it make no sense to say (A + B)/2 = 3/2. But, when numeric grades are used, the temptation to apply arithmetic operations is too great to resist and most of us will readily accept that (1 + 2)/2 = 1.5 and try to argue sense into this meaningless number.

Equating numeric and letter grades: Admitted, writing letter grades (A, B. C, etc.) may be clumsier than writing numeric grades (1, 2, 3, etc.).

So, for convenience, numeric grades are always used in place where letter grades should appear. Here, we are likely to fall into the trap of equating *ordinal numbers* (positioning numbers, 1st, 2nd, 3rd, etc.) with *cardinal numbers* (counting numbers, *one, two three*, etc) simply because the two sets of numbers look the same (1, 2, 3. etc.). In other words, we erroneously transfer the function of one set of number to the other (where it does not apply).

Levels of measurement: In measurement theory, data in numeric form has four levels: nominal, ordinal, interval, and ratio. GPA in the form of numeric grades are actually codes for letter grades and they function at the ordinal level of measurement (or form an ordinal scale) and the permissible arithmetic operations are < and >, not even + and −, not to mention × and ÷. This being the case, two numeric grades for the same or different courses cannot be legitimately added or subtracted, let alone multiplied or divided. Two numeric grades for the same course can be meaningfully compared as better or worse, but how much better or worse is not really known. Two numeric grades for different courses should not be compared even, because the course have different qualities or characteristics. Unfortunately, such conceptual blunders are common and have been accepted, and worldwide at that!

Unequal difference: As pointed out above, the difference between two adjacent grades is in fact unknown or ill-defined. Even when the grades are converted to marks, the mark ranges are different. This being the case, comparing two adjacent grades may not have the same meaning. For instance, in the American system, A(4)[80–100], B(3)[70–79], C(2)[60–69], D(1)[50–59], F(0)[0–49]. Thus, a GPA difference of one grade between A and B cover 20 marks, but the difference of also one grade between B and C covers only 10 marks. Things can get more complicated when several courses are compared.

Meanings of decimal values: Because numeric grades are more convenient than letter grades and grades of 1, 2, 3, etc., are too coarse while administration (e.g., pass/fail, selection for programmes) always need finer information, decimal values are used. Thus, conventionally, the best GPA is 4.00 and a poorer one may be 3.75 and even poorer may be 3.70, with differences of 0.25 and 0.05. This creates an impression that GPA is very precise (reliable) and accurate (valid): the system does not allow ambiguity; the professor or administrator are 'strict in maintaining standard'. From the measurement perspective, such precision and accuracy are more imagined than real, for the simple reason that educational measures are highly fallible, for instance, the same essay marked twice by the same professor with a time interval is likely to get different grades or marks and the same essay marked by different professors are bound to get different grades or marks, too. When such variation in assessment occurs, decimal values have practical no value as it does not represent anything both substantively and substantially.

Mutual compensation: When numeric grades for different courses are added together to derive the GPA, the tacit assumption is that the courses are mutually compensatory. This means that weakness in some courses can be compensated by strengths in other courses. This may not always be true. A students strong in language but weak in mathematics is quite different from one who is strong in mathematics but weak in language. If they have the same GPA and are admitted to the same programme which heavily rely on one of the two subjects, one of them is not going to do well because of the mismatch of ability and course demand. Thus, assuming mutual compensation of courses can be very costly for the individuals as well as the systems.

International incomparability: Cross-nation study has become very common nowadays and GPA are always required and used for cross-nation admission. Unfortunately, different nations have different mark ranges for the GPA. To illustrate, Table 1 shows the mark ranges for USA, Russia, and Korea.

Table 1. Mark Ranges for USA, Russia, and Korea

USA	F[0–49]	D[50–59]	C[60–69]	B[70–79]	A[80–100]
Russia	F[0–25]	D[26–49]	C[50–74]	B[75–84]	A[85–100]
Korea	F[0–59]	D[60–69]	C[70–79]	B[80–90]	A[90–100]

Take the grade of C. Obviously, taken at face value, the "average" students from the three countries are of different calibers. The Korean is definitely better than the American and Russian, but the Russian could be better or worse than the American. Look at the best students with a GPA of A. It is hardest to be such a student in Korea, somewhat easier in Russia, and easiest in USA.

What about the GPA systems of Singapore universities? Table 2 below shows for the National University of Singapore (NUS), the Nanyang Technological University (NTU), and the Singapore Management University (SMU) (http://digitalsenior.sg/gpa-system/). Obviously, it is harder to get an A in NUS and NTU than in SMU. The same goes for B and C grades, though not as hard as for A.

Table 2.   GPA Systems of Three Universities in Singapore

NUS & NTU	F[0.00]	D[1.00–1.50]	C[2.00–2.50]	B[3.00–4.00]	A[4.50–5.00]
SMU	F[0.00] (49 and below)	D[1.00–1.30] (50–59)	C[1.70–2.30] (60–69)	B[2.70–3.30] (70–79)	A[3.70–4.30] (80 and above)

Note: A, B, C each has three sub-grades (e.g., A+, A, A–); D has two (D+, D).

It is interesting to note that the highest GPS is 4.00 in most countries but it is 5.00 for NUS and NTU. One wonders how the higher GPA has been received and treated when NUS and NTU graduates with full GPA seek to do postgraduate study in other countries. One also wonders how foreign students of NUS and NTU who obtained the highest GPA are received when they are back in their countries.

Conclusion

GPA in the form of numeric grade is a convenient administrative device as it is supposed to summarize a student's performance in a combination of courses. Being one numeric, it makes decisions such as admission and selection easier than Credit*Points for several courses. This convenience comes with a price as the student's relative strengths and weaknesses are "averaged out" and such important information is lost. When using GPA, caution against such over-simplification is advisable and school leaders, teachers, and parents need to be aware of the pitfall of GPA. More discussion on the relevant issues can be found in Soh (2011).

References

Hartman, T., Jaksa, P. & Pallandina, L.J. (2000). *Thom Hartman's Complete Guide to ADHD*. Underwood Books. Retrieved July 30, 2010, from http:// professionals.collegeboard.com/profdownload/pdf/RR%2088-11.PDF.

Soh, Kay Cheng (2011). Grade point average: what's wrong and what's the alternative? *Journal of Higher Education Policy and Management*, 33(1), 27–36.

15. What Is Assessment Literacy?

Although this book is about assessment literacy (not the whole book but much of it), we have not discussed it formally, not even referring to the term. This, of course, is intentional, and what we have talked about up till this point is, in fact, a preparation for this chapter.

A decade ago, the highly regarded American assessment expert W. James Popham (2006) made the following statement about teachers (politely referred to as *educators*) in the USA:

> What most of today's educators know about education assessment would fit comfortably inside a kindergartner's half-filled milk carton. This is astonishing in light of the fact that during the last 25 years, educator competence has been increasingly determined by student performance on various large-scale examinations... A profession's adequacy is being judged on the basis of tools that the profession's members don't understand. This situation is analogous to asking doctors and nurses to do their jobs without knowing how to interpret patient charts...

Saying so, Popham was literally asking: Would you trust a cardiologist who does not know how to read an ECG graph? Likewise, would you trust a teacher who does not know how to interpret exam results?

Importance of assessment literacy

There is no better way to emphasize the importance of assessment literacy than what Popham did by drawing the parallelism between the medical and teaching professions. Medical practitioners depend on test results of all kind to guide them in diagnosis and prescription when treating patients. Analogously, teachers depend on exam results of various types to make decisions on how to best help students learn. Without such information and proper interpretation, the doctors and the teachers are doing their respective jobs with a short-gun approach — hastily using a wide range of techniques that are nonselective and haphazard though with the hope of hitting the right target.

Popham went further to say that not only do teachers need assessment literacy but everyone else who has an interest in children's education, and this *everyone* includes school leaders, policy-makers, and parents, besides teachers.

In the past, assessment tools were crafted by test specialists while teachers were passive users. This is true in the American context where standardized tests are the regular fixture of the school. Nowadays, *with the emphasis on assessment for learning* (or *formative* assessment) in contrast with *assessment of learning* (or *summative* assessment), teachers, in America and elsewhere, are expected to use assessment in a more engaged manner to help students learn. Teachers are therefore expected to use test information not only for assessment *of* learning (i.e., deciding who has done well) but also, perhaps more importantly, assessment *for* learning (i.e., deciding who needs help and how to help). This shift of emphasis all the more underlines the importance of the teacher's assessment literacy.

Moreover, student learning is now not totally entrusted to the teachers or thrusted into the hands of teachers; school leaders also play a role in guiding teachers and school-based curricular revision. Besides, it is now recognized that parents also play a role in their children's learning. Thus, for the school leaders and parents to contribute to student learning, they need to have reliable and valid exam results and also need to be able to properly interpret and hence use them. This is to say, not only teachers but also school leaders and parents need assessment literacy. In this sense, assessment literacy is a common platform for teachers, school leaders, and parents where shared understanding and responsibility prevail for the benefit of the children.

Measuring assessment literacy

There have been a number of efforts to measure assessment literacy, particularly of teachers. In a systematic review of studies in assessment literacy from 1991 to 2012, 36 measures were covered, showing the keen interest of researchers in this new field of educational measurement. In other words, there are a multitude of assessment standards across the world and numerous assessment literacy measures that represent different conceptions of assessment literacy.

Assessment literacy is the term first used by Rick Stiggins in 1991 referring to teachers' understanding of the differences between sound and unsound assessment procedures and use of assessment outcomes. Assessment literate teachers are expected to have a clear understanding of the purposes and targets of assessment, the competence in choosing appropriate assessment procedures, the capability of conducting assessment effectively and avoiding pit-falls in the process of assessment practices and interpretation of assessment results.

These expectation sound simple but they can be a tall order in reality. However, according to Popham, increasing numbers of professional development programs have dealt with assessment literacy for teachers and school leaders. Such programmes deal mainly with two functions of assessment: (1) classroom assessments and (2) accountability assessments. He concluded that assessment literacy is a *sine qua non* for today's competent teachers and must be a pivotal content area for current and future staff development endeavors. Nonetheless, Popham who is vehement about the lack of assessment literacy among American teachers has a simple expectation, thus,

> When I refer to assessment literacy, I'm not thinking about a large collection of abstruse notions unrelated to the day-to-day decisions that educators face. On the contrary, assessment-literate educators need to understand a relatively small number of commonsense measurement fundamentals, not a stack of psychometric exotica.

To-date, Mertler & Campbell's adaptation of Plake and Impara's *Teacher Assessment Literacy Questionnaire* is the most popular measure of assessment literacy of teachers. It comprises 35 items measuring teachers' general concepts about testing and assessment. The items take the fore of seven scenarios featuring teachers who were facing various assessment-related decisions. Shown below is a sample item and it deals with the measurement concept of score validity:

Which of the following grading practices results in a grade that **least** reflects students' achievement?

○ Mr. Jones requires students to turn in homework; however, he only grades the odd numbered items.

○ Mrs. Brown uses weekly quizzes and three major examinations to assign final grades in her class.

○ Ms. Smith permits students to redo their assignments several times if they need more opportunities to meet her standards for grades.

○ Miss Engle deducts 5 points from a student's test grade for disruptive behavior.

The *Classroom Assessment Literacy Inventory* followed *The Standards for Teacher Competence in the Educational Assessment of Students,* which was a joint effort of the American Federation of Teachers, the National Council on Measurement in Education, and the National Education Association. The collaboration of these organizations evidences that assessment literacy is taken very seriously. Seven such standards were adopted, resulting in items measuring the following seven aspects of assessment literacy:

1. Choosing Appropriate Assessment Methods
2. Developing Appropriate Assessment Methods
3. Administering, Scoring, and Interpreting the Results of Assessments
4. Using Assessment Results to Make Decisions
5. Developing Valid Grading Procedures
6. Communicating Assessment Results
7. Recognizing Unethical or Illegal Practices

It stands to reason that these seven aspects are intimately relevant to the teachers' day-to-day assessment responsibilities and that it is reasonable to expect all teachers to be equipped with the attendant understanding and skills.

Singapore context

In recent years, the Singapore Ministry of Education has launched the initiatives emphasizing higher-order thinking skills and deep understanding in teaching, such as "Teach Less, Learn More" and "Thinking Schools, Learning Nations". Consequently, teachers are required to make changes to their assessment practice and to equip themselves with sufficient assessment literacy.

In systems like that of the USA where standardized tests are designed by test specialists through long and arduous process of test development, applying sophisticated psychometric concepts and principles and with regular intermittent revisions, it is reasonable to assume that the resultant assessment tools made available to the teacher are of a high psychometric quality. In that case, the most critical aspect of assessment literacy teachers need is to have the ability to properly interpret the test results they obtain through administering the tests. Measurement knowledge beyond this is good to have but not critically needed.

In contrast, however, in a system like that of Singapore, where standardized tests are *not* an omnipresent fixture, teacher-made tests are almost the only assessment tool available. This indicates that the teachers need to have assessment literacy of a much broader range, going beyond just interpretation of test results.

Domains of assessment literacy

What then are the understanding and skills teachers need to have for assessment literacy. The traditional definition of *literacy* refers to the ability to read, write, and do arithmetic. By extension, assessment literacy would mean the ability to read, write, and do arithmetic with concepts and skills related to assessment. To be able to do this the teachers should be able to handle assessment-related discourse which may involve some numeric concepts. However, this does not require a highly academic and theoretical competence which include advanced level statistics. In other words, assessment literacy is at a level like literacy among literate people, as contrasted with the expertise and sophistication of literary people such as novelists, poets, playwrights who have highly developed command of language and relevant prowess's.

What then are the specific understanding and skills that make up assessment literacy?

Firstly, teachers need to have an understanding of the nature and functions of assessment if they, as professionals, are to do things not blindly but knowing why they are doing. Such understanding enables them to know why they are doing what they are (or expected) to do, so that they do not do them blindly with no meaningful purposes. It may be argued that doing things with proper understanding of the purposes is a hallmark of being professionals.

Secondly, teachers need the practical skills to design and use a variety of item formats to meet the instructional needs in their daily work and such needs vary with the content of the subjects and student abilities. Such skills may not be needed when standardized tests are available for summative assessment (as in the American context), but they are critical in the present day Singapore context when teachers are expected to craft their own exams to assess and monitor student learning for formative assessment.

Thirdly, once teachers have obtained exam results, they need to be able to properly interpret the scores or other results to inform further teaching and guide student learning. Obtaining test scores without being able to properly interpret them is analogous to the situation depicted in the quote from Popham at the beginning of this chapter — health professionals unable to interpret patient charts.

Finally, they need to be able to evaluate the qualities of the exam results, and this entails knowledge of *basic* statistics. This, unfortunately, is what many teachers try to avoid, due mainly to lack of training. Such knowledge enable teachers to see assessment results in proper light, knowing their functions as well as their limitations in terms of measurement error which is an inherent part of educational assessment. Without an understanding of such concepts of reliability and validity, teachers tend to take assessment results too literally and may make inappropriate conclusions about students and their learning and may even make unwarranted decisions.

Concluding note

While the above may be seen as a professional competency required of teachers, admittedly, it may not be realistic and necessary for school leaders and parents to be as knowledgeable and sophisticated as teachers where assessment literacy is concerned. Such knowledge, however, enables school leaders and parents to understand why teachers do what they do and whether they are doing them right. This is good for mutual understanding that enables the three parties to work more closely and amicably for the good of the students (or children).

16. How Assessment Literate Are You?

In this very last chapter, you find a set of 40 MCQ questions. They come in four sets of 10 with each set focusing on one of the four domains (or aspects) of assessment literacy mentioned in the previous chapter.

Having come this far reading this book, you should be able to answer correctly most of the questions, though not all. Give them (or your good self) a trial. For this, you need to photocopy the Answer Sheet to record your choices for the options. Once you have answered all the questions, check your answers against the Scoring Keys and count the number of correct answers for each set.

Some concepts of assessment literacy are not very different from common sense, others require specific training. If you do well in those of the former kind, that's great; it shows that you are thinking in the right direction. If you do not do well in the latter kind, that is fine; it simply means you have not been trained, but you may want to learn.

Here we go.

Assessment Literacy Scale

Subtest 1: Nature and Function of Assessment

Item	Option For each item, choose one of the four options and enter your choice in the Answer Sheet.
1. What is the most important function of assessing students?	1. To inform parents about the children's achievement 2. To assure school that teachers teach diligently 3. Let students know their achievement and areas to improve 4. Prepare students for large-scale external exams
2. How can teachers use testing results to help students continuously improve their achievement?	1. Use test results for formative assessment. 2. Use test results for summative assessment. 3. Use above-level testing to challenge students. 4. Use below-level testing to encourage students.
3. Which of these is NOT an educational function of assessment?	1. To promote motivation 2. To enhance students' psychological condition 3. To ensure over-learning 4. To make choices
4. Which of these is NOT a direct function of assessment?	1. To evaluate students 2. To evaluate teachers 3. To evaluate the curriculum 4. To determine individual talent
5. What can assessment results be used for?	1. To diagnose students' learning difficulties 2. To understand the effectiveness of teaching 3. To find out the effects of curriculum changes 4. All of the above
6. To help students make progress, which is the best thing to do after assessment?	1. Tell the class its average mark. 2. Tell the class the highest and lowest marks. 3. Name the best and the worst students. 4. Let each student know his errors.
7. Which is the most important function of class tests?	1. Draw parents' attention to students' learning. 2. Let students know their strengths and weaknesses. 3. To provide a mark when a student has missed an exam. 4. To ensure the students' results are not entirely dependent on exams.

(Continued)

Subtest 1 (*Continued*)

Item	Option For each item, choose one of the four options and enter your choice in the Answer Sheet.
8. To compare a student's score with those of his classmates. What kind of assessment is this?	1. Formative assessment 2. Summative assessment 3. Criterion-referenced assessment 4. Norm-referenced assessment
9. Using test scores to decide whether students have reached the expected standard. What kind of assessment is this?	1. Formative assessment 2. Summative assessment 3. Criterion-referenced assessment 4. Norm-referenced assessment
10. When using assessment to diagnose students' learning difficulties, how difficult should the items be?	1. Highly difficult 2. Very easy 3. Moderately difficult 4. Mixture of easy and difficult items

Subtest 2: Design and Use of Test Items

Item	Option For each item, choose one of the four options and enter your choice in the Answer Sheet
11. What is the most important advantage of multiple-choice items?	1. Easy to mark 2. Marking is objective 3. Variation in design 4. Systematic setting
12. Which language ability is most suited to multiple-choice items?	1. Oral interaction 2. Written interaction 3. Sentence construction 4. Word comprehension
13. Which language ability is most suited to scrambled sentence?	1. Reading comprehension 2. Mastery of vocabulary 3. Punctuations 4. Written expression
14. Asking students to write their own answers in reading comprehension. What is the weakness of this testing?	1. Too much time to write. 2. Too much time to mark. 3. Poor reliability 4. Poor validity

(*Continued*)

Subtest 2 (*Continued*)

Item	Option **For each item, choose one of the four options and enter your choice in the Answer Sheet**
15. What is cloze procedure best for assessing?	1. Reading comprehension 2. Knowledge of grammar 3. Sentence construction 4. Word recognition speed
16. To assess students' written expression, which arrangement yields highvalidity?	1. Ask students to write three short essays, each of 100 words. 2. Ask students to write a long essay of 300 words. 3. Ask students to complete three cloze passages, each of 100 words. 4. As students to complete a cloze passage of 300 words.
17. Objective items and essay-type questions both have strengths and weaknesses. Which is NOT a strength of objective items?	1. Broad coverage of content 2. Fixed marking standard 3. Suited tp many language abilities 4. Assessing students' ability in organization
18. When assessing students' written expression by asking them to write on specified topic, which is the most critical factor?	1. Student' knowledge of essay structure 2. Students' relevant life experience 3. The required length of the essay 4. Students' mastery of punctuations
19. When assessing students' written expression by asking them to write on specified topic, how should the topic be?	1. No sex bias 2. No racial bias 3. No socioeconomic bias 4. All of the above
20. When assessing students' written expression by asking them to write on specified topic, what is the greatest DISADVANTAGE?	1. Students may not know enough about the topic. 2. Students are always poor in vocabulary 3. Teachers need to spend much time marking. 4. Teachers' subjectivity affects marking.

Subtest 3: Interpretation of Test Results

Item	Option For each item, choose one of the four options and enter your choice in the Answer Sheet
21. A good multiple-choice item should have how many percent of students answering correctly?	1. 80–100% 2. 60–80% 3. 40–60% 4. 20–40%
22. A good multiple-choice items should have which MINIMUM ratio of percent students answering correctly and wrongly?	1. 80% correct, 20% wrong 2. 60% correct, 40% wrong 3. 50% correct, 50% wrong 4. 40% correct, 60% wrong
23. What is the most important quality of options of a multiple-choice item?	1. Options should be obviously different 2. Options should NOT be too different. 3. Options should be arranged logically. 4. Options and item stem should be grammatically consistent.
24. A multiple-choice item has about the same proportion of students answering correctly and wrongly. What does this show?	1. The item is very well-crafted. 2. The item has low discrimination power. 3. The item discriminates adequately. 4. The item has an adequate difficulty level.
25. Allowing student to choose topics for writing essay — what is the most serious problem of doing so?	1. The topics may not be of the same difficulty. 2. Too many choices make students unsure. 3. Different content requires too much of the teacher's time. 4. The teacher's preference will influence marking.
26. A student obtained 75 marks for a test. How good is this mark?	1. It is a poor mark. 2. It is a good mark. 3. It is a mediocre mark. 4. Insufficient information, cannot be interpreted.
27. A student obtained49 marks for a test. The passing mark is 50. The teachers insists that the student has failed the test. What does this mean?	1. The teachers is serious about marks. 2. The teachers has no idea of measurement error. 3. The teacher is not sympathetic toward the student. 4. The teachers is not willing to speak for the student.

(Continued)

Subtest 3 (*Continued*)

Item	Option For each item, choose one of the four options and enter your choice in the Answer Sheet
28. The PSLE uses T-scores for reporting. What kind of scores are T-scores?	1. Raw marks students deserve. 2. Raw marks based on predetermined standards. 3. Standardized scores for a standardized test. 4. Standard scores based on standard deviations.
29. A student obtained a T-score of 60 for an exam. How good was the student?	1. He was better than 60% of his classmates. 2. He answered correctly 60% of the test items. 3. He was better than 84% of his classmates. 4. He answered correctly 84 items.
30. A student got a mark of 60 last month and 75 this month for the tests. Hs he improved?	1. He has improved by 15 marks. 2. He has gained 15 positions. 3. He has improved by 25%. 4. Insufficient information, cannot interpret.

Subtest 4: Reliability, Validity and Basic Statistics

Item	Option For each item, choose one of the four options and enter your choice in the Answer Sheet
31. A teachers assessed her P3 class using a P5 test. What will happen to the test results?	1. Low reliability, high validity. 2. High reliability, low validity. 3. Reliability and validity are both high. 4. Reliability and validity are both low.
32. Mr. Zhang assessed his P5 class using a P3 test. What will happen to the test results?	1. Low reliability, high validity. 2. High reliability, low validity. 3. Reliability and validity are both high. 4. Reliability and validity are both low.
33. Mr. Zhang and Ms. Li marked the same set of homework independently. Each student got very different marks for the same homework. What does this mean?	1. The marks given by the teachers have low reliability. 2. The marks given by the teachers have high reliability. 3. The marks given by the teachers have low validity. 4. The marks given by the teachers have high validity.

(*Continued*)

Subtest 4 (*Continued*)

Item	Option For each item, choose one of the four options and enter your choice in the Answer Sheet.
34. Ms. Zhang assessed his students using a test of 20 items. For each student, there was mark for the first 10 items and another for the last 10 items. She intended to check whether the two sets of marks are consistent. What was she checking?	1. She was checking the reliability of the marks. 2. She was checking the validity of the marks. 3. She was checking the reliability and validity of the marks. 4. She was checking the difficulty levels of the two sets of items.
35. The reliability and validity of assessment results are related. What kind of a relation is there?	1. Low reliability and high validity. 2. Low reliability and low validity. 3. High reliability and low validity. 4. All of the above are possible.
36. Which mark of the following is the mode? 2, 2, 2, 3, 3, 6, 9, 13, 21	1. 2 2. 6 3. 9 4. 21
37. What kind of distribution do the following marks form? 2, 2, 2, 3, 3, 6, 9, 13, 21	1. Normal distribution 2. Balanced distribution 3. Positively skewed distribution 4. Negatively skewed distribution
38. When a set of marks form a normal distribution, which is the best central tendency?	1. Mode 2. Median 3. Mean 4. All of the above
39. A set of marks has a very large standard deviation. What does this indicate?	1. Students got marks that were very different from the passing mark. 2. Students got marks that were very close to the passing mark. 3. Students performed very differently. 4. Students had very little differences.
40. Students' achievement and attitude for learning have a correlation of r = 0.5. What does this indicate?	1. Learning attitude is influenced by achievement up to 25%. 2. Achievement is influenced by learning attitude up to 25%. 3. Achievement and learning attitude have 25% of mutual influence. 4. Achievement and learning attitude have 50% of mutual influence.

Answer Sheet

Subtest 1		Subtest 2		Subtest 3		Subtest 4	
Item	Answer	Item	Answer	Item	Answer	Item	Answer
1		11		21		31	
2		12		22		32	
3		13		23		33	
4		14		24		34	
5		15		25		35	
6		16		26		36	
7		17		27		37	
8		18		28		38	
9		19		29		39	
10		20		30		40	
Subtotal		Subtotal		Subtotal		Subtotal	
Grand total							

Answer Keys

Subtest 1		Subtest 2		Subtest 3		Subtest 4	
Item	**Answer**	Item	**Answer**	Item	**Answer**	Item	**Answer**
1	3	11	2	21	3	31	2
2	1	12	4	22	4	32	2
3	4	13	1	23	2	33	1
4	2	14	4	24	2	34	1
5	4	15	1	25	1	35	2
6	4	16	1	26	4	36	1
7	2	17	4	27	2	37	3
8	4	18	2	28	4	38	4
9	3	19	4	29	3	39	3
10	2	20	4	30	4	40	3

Scores and Interpretation

As discussed in an earlier chapter, the two major approaches to score interpretation are (1) norm-referenced and (2) criterion-referenced.

Norm-referenced interpretation compares a person's test score with the scores of all who have taken the same test and presents the results in terms of a percentile, indicating how far ahead the person having the test score stands among the peers. For instance, a score of 81th percentile indicates that the person is better than 80% of his peers.

On the other hand, *criterion-referenced interpretation* compares a person's test score again a pre-determined cut-score (passing mark), disregarding where he stands among the peers. Once the test score matches the cut-score, he is considered as having passed the test; and, it does not matter how far above the cut-score — he simply passes.

This sounds simple but in fact setting cut-score is a difficult measurement task, because arbitrarily setting a passing mark (e.g., 50%, 75%, etc.) does not work. It requires empirical verification before the use of the test. Basically, this entails finding which of several potential cut-scores work best in identifying those who can really benefit from the next higher level of learning. If the test is suitable for a particular class level, the convention is that 90% of the students tested should be able to answer correctly 90% of the items; thus, giving 81% of correct response. Therefore, it seems that 80% correct response is a reasonable cut-score. With this in mind, the following score ranges may serve as a guide for you to assess how assessment literate you are after taken the test above.

Subtest score	Classification	Remarks	Whole test score
10	Excellent	You are almost perfectly literate in assessment.	39–40
9	Good	You are quite literate in assessment	36–38
8	Pass	You have the required minimum assessment literacy	32–35
7	Borderline	You are somewhat weak in assessment literacy	28–31
6 or less	Weak	You are obviously weak in assessment literacy	24 or less

The above is suggested for teachers who, as professionals involving in assessment practically every day (just like medical doctors with patients), need thorough (or almost so) understanding and competence. However, for school leaders and parents, a lower cut-score is reasonable — they need to know but not to the extent of teachers. In view of such differences, an adjusted scheme of classification is suggested below:

Subtest score	Teacher	School leaders	Parents	Whole test score
10	Excellent			39–40
9	Good	Excellent	Excellent	36–38
8	Pass	Good		32–35
7	Borderline	Pass	Good	28–31
6	Weak	Borderline	Pass	24–27
5		Weak	Borderline	20–23
4 or less			Weak	Less than 20

The four subtests are not of equal demand. Subtests 1 deals with understanding of the nature and functions of assessment; these are non-technical and can be acquired through experience and clear thinking. It should therefore be the easiest of the four domains and higher scores can be expected.

Subtests 2 and 3 cover some technical aspects of exam preparation and interpretation of exam results. Although some of the concepts are still commonsensical, specific training helps. The items in these two subtests are therefore somewhat more difficult than those in Subtest 1. For this reason, high score cannot be expected from the uninitiated, although moderate score can be a reasonable expectation.

Subtest 4 covers concepts which are essential to educational measurement (and hence exams). Such concepts of reliability and validity and some basic statistics needed for score interpretation are not common sense and have to be specifically trained. For this reason, low scores are expected of the uninitiated. Even people who have had the relevant training in this domain sometimes do not score high; they might have not learned well or have not been taught well, or both.

Nevertheless, bearing in mind the differences among the subtests, you can have a realistic evaluation of your assessment literacy.

Endnote

In the later 1970s, I was the sole editor of a monthly magazine, *Teachers' Forum*, published by the Ministry of Education, Singapore. I took the opportunity to share ideas with teachers about assessment by writing a short article each month. There articles were later compiled into *On Assessment: Ten Talks for Educational Practitioners*. This booklet was so widely read by trainee-teachers at the then Institute of Education that the covers were literally torn. My friend Dr. Quek Khiok Seng who ran an assessment course there kept encouraging me to have a re-issue but I, for some unknown reasons, just could not make it. Decades passed by. *On Assessment* has since became the core of the present book which expands on the main ideas thereof, with additional chapters emerging from the recent trends and concerns such as exam stress, creativity, project work, assessment rubrics, and above-level testing.

Education in Singapore has seen tremendous transformation with plentiful new ideas tried out and then given up to be followed by more try-outs. However, assessment seems to be a constant, even the only constant, and, with it, the level of assessment literacy among educational practitioners which seems to stand still. A minority of teachers have specialized training in assessment, the majority have some introductory briefings on assessment but mostly educate themselves by learning on the job. In view of the importance placed on assessment in Singapore schools, this is an irony. It is therefore hoped that this book will fill the vacuum and help to rectify the situation.

A personal note. In the midst of finalizing the manuscript, my wife, Lee Piak Geok @ Lee Peck Geok passed on, after two major operations within six months at the age of early eighties. My painful loss held up the progress before I could pick up myself and the book. All these years, her encouragement and understanding have been a sources of strength to my professional pursuits. Perhaps, there is no better way I can express my love and gratitude than publishing this book in memory of her.

SKC

11 March 2016

Appendix A: Statistical Concepts Plainly Explained

Central Tendency: A set of exam scores has several statistical characteristics. The first important one is the central tendency, indicating a score towards which the scores congregate; this is analogous to the centre of gravity of an object. As the scores vary from low to high, a score is needed to represent the distribution. Calculation of the statistics is usually entrusted to the computer (e.g., using *Excel*), the formulas (some look rather formidable) will not be included here and the focus is understanding of the relevant concepts.

Mean: This is more accurately called the *arithmetic mean* and is often referred to as the *average,* although there are several averages. The mean is often, though not all the time, used to represent a set of scores to indicate the general level of performance on an exam of a class or level. When we analyze and discuss exam results, we more often than not use the mean.

For example, a group of ten students obtained the following scores for an exam which had 30 as its full-mark:

15 18 20 19 18 18 22 21 23 18

When we add up these ten scores, the total is 192. Since the total belongs to ten students, we divide it by ten to get the mean (average) of 19.2. Note that none of the students actually got a score of 19.2. This is an abstraction indicating that *on average a student will score 19.2*. Or, to put it in another way, *a typical student of the group will score 19.2*.

The mean makes it possible for us to think of just one score instead of ten 'different' scores when reporting or discussing the students' performance.

Mode: This is *most frequent score* in a set of scores. If we go by the majority, this most frequent score (mode) is a legitimate representative the whole set of scores. Although the modes does not have the precision the mean has, it is a quick-and-rough indication of general level of performance.

In the above example, 18 appears four times and no other scores do. So, 18 is the mode to represent the set of ten scores. However, when there are many scores, there may be two or more equally frequent scores, then the distribution is said to be *bimodal* or *multi-modal*.

Median: This is middle-most score in a distribution when the scores are arranged in ascending (or descending) order when there are *odd* number of scores. However, for *even* number of scores, the average of the middle-most two score is the median. In a sense, the median is a very real centre of a set of scores. The median separates the distribution into two equal halves.

If we arrange the above ten scores in ascending order, we get:

15 18 18 18 18 19 20 21 22 23

Here, the two middle-most scores are 18 and 19, and their average is 18.5 and this is the median which divides the distribution into two equal halves, with five scores below 18.5 and another five scores above this.

The median is most useful to represent a set of scores when there are outliers (extremely low or high scores) because of its stability (i.e., not affected by outliers). For example, there is an extremely high score in the set:

15 18 18 18 18 19 20 21 22 **30**

For this set of scores, the mean is 19.9 but the median remains as 18.5. In this case, the mean over-estimated the performance and the median is therefore a more appropriate representative of the scores.

On the other hand, when there is an extremely low score like these:

2 18 18 18 18 19 20 21 22 23

For these, the mean is 17.9 but the median remains at 18.5. In this case, the mean under-estimated the performance and the median is therefore a more appropriate representative of the scores.

Percent: This is a very commonly used term when reporting or discussing exam results. *Percent* simply mean "of 100 subdivisions" and is often coded as %.

Percent score: Exam results are often reported and discussed in terms of percent score. This in fact is converting the full-mark (whatever it is) as if the scale has 100 points. A student's score is then converted to a certain percent.

For example, a 30-item exam has a full-mark of 30. Thus, answering an item correctly carries one mark which, when converted, is equivalent to 3.3(%). A score of 15 then is reported as 15/30 (×100%) or 50 percent, that is, half of the full-mark. Likewise, a score of 30 is reported as 30/30 (×100%) or 100 percent, all of the full-mark.

Be watchful when percent score is reported as it tends to create an impression of importance. For example, if an exam has only ten items, getting three items right yields a percent score of 30, which look impressive.

Percentile: While percent score refers to the proportion a score is of full-mark, a percentile indicates where a student stands on a 100-position scale, in terms of the proportion of scores (students) *a given score is better than.*

For example, a score of 18 (in the above set of scores) has a percentile of 60th, and this indicates that there are 60% of other possible scores below it. Likewise, a score of 21 has a percentile of 70th and this indicates that there are 70% of other scores below it.

Variability: The second most important statistical characteristic of a set of score is its variability — how widely spreading out the scores are from the centre (be it the mean or median). Two classes of students may have the same means but different variability and hence the classes are different in the assessed ability.

Range: This is an indication of how widely the scores are spreading. It is calculated as the difference between the lowest and the highest scores in a set. The greater the range, the wider the spread, indicating that the students are more heterogeneous.

For example, in the first set of scores, the lowest is 15 and the highest 23, so the range is 8. The ranges for the second and the third sets of scores above are, 15 and 21 respectively. Of course, as you might have noticed, the range is sensitive to outlier which can change it drastically. Compare the first and the third sets and you will realize this.

Standard deviation: This is the most frequently used indication of variability of a set of scores. Like the range, the greater the standard deviation (SD), the wider the spread of scores and the more heterogeneous the students. The calculation of SD involves several computational steps and hence is always trusted to the computer.

For example, the first set of scores has SD = 2.35, the second set SD = 4.04, and the third set SD = 5.88. Obviously, these SDs reflect the different spreads of the three sets of scores.

Score Distribution: Exam scores vary from very low to very high, spreading over a wide range on a continuum. Usually, there are much more scores in the middle and fewer as the scores get higher and lower. When the number of scores (students) are many, the scores form one kind of distribution called the *normal distribution*. However, depending on the facilities (F-indices) of the test items, the scores may form a *skewed distribution*.

Normal distribution: This is often referred to as the bell-shaped distribution curve, because of how it looks (see Figure A1). The distribution is symmetrical; if you fold the curve in the middle, the two sides of the curve overlap. When there is a large number of students taking an exam that suits their ability, the scores mostly likely form such a curve.

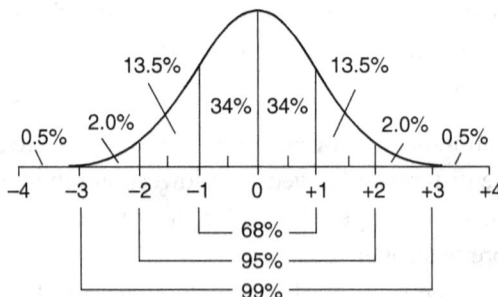

Figure A1.   The normal curve

The normal curve can be divided into six sectors, using the SD. This results in three sectors below the mean and three above. Theoretically, the two sectors around the mean each covers 34% of the cases; thus, if 120 students have taken the exam, there will be 82 (68%) students of them scoring between one SD below the mean and one SD above the mean. Thus, if the mean is 40 and the SD 8, then the middle-most 68% (82) students will score no less than 32 and not more than 48. By tradition, these middle-most 68% students are considered as 'normal'. [Note that 'Normal' as used in Singapore context has a different meaning.]

On the high side, the next sector contains 14%, leaving 2% at the top end; these are the able or supra-normal students. On the low side, the same thing happens and the students are considered as less able or sub-normal.

Skewed distribution: When an exam is very easy, more students are likely to get high scores which then form a negatively skewed distribution (also called left-skewed distribution) as shown on the left side of Figure A2.

On the other hand, when an exam is very difficult, more students are likely to get low scores which then form a positively skewed distribution (also called right-skewed distribution) as shown on the right side of Figure A2.

Note the positions of the mean, the median, and the mode. In each curve, the mode indicates the most frequent score, the mean is nearer to the tail end, and the median in between the mode and the mean.

In the case, of a negatively (left) skewed distribution, the mean is rather low, thus under-estimating the performance and the median is higher, more realistically representing the performance. The opposite is true for a

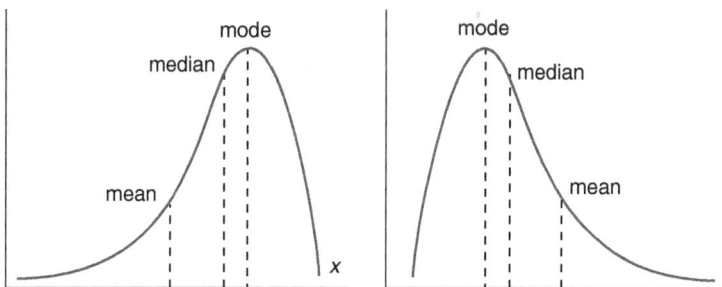

Figure A2. Skewed distributions

positively (right) skewed distribution. Hence, when distribution is skewed, the median is a better indicator than the mean.

Correlation: Correlation indicates the pattern of change of two set of exam scores obtained from one and the same groups of students. The two sets of scores for the same students may increase in tandem (positive correlation), decrease in tandem (negative correlation), or have no consistent pattern (no correlation). The magnitude of correlation coefficient vary from +1.00 (perfect positive correlation) to −1.00 (perfect negative correlation). And, when the two sets of score do not correlate, the correlation coefficient is 0.00. Figure A3 depict these three situations.

Correlation (Pearson): Pearson's product moment correlation coefficient (r) is calculated using the scores which are continuous. The squared-r (r^2) indicates the extent to which the two variables overlap and is called coefficient of determination, with the assumption that one variables is causing the other to change.

For example, a Pearson's $r = 0.70$ is found between students' exam scores for English Language and Mother Tongue Language, then the two languages are said to have 49 percent overlap (all rounding up to 50 percent).

However, remember that correlation is bi-directional, ability in one subject may influence ability in another subject and **vice versa**, and it is always not possible to say with certainty which is causing which, because causality is not a statistical but logical concept (beyond the exam scores).

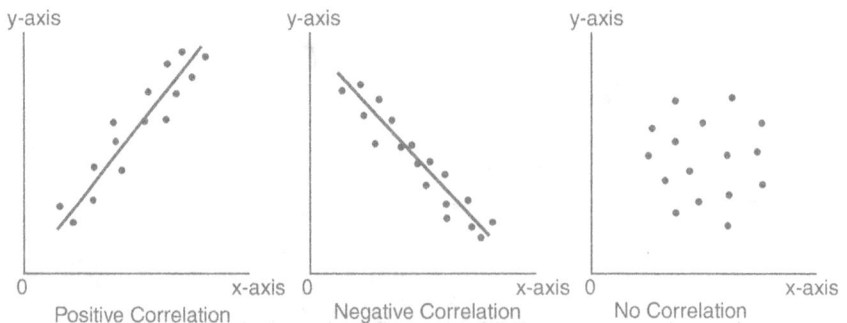

Figure A3.   Patterns of Correlation

Correlation (Spearman): Spearman's rank order correlation coefficient (ρ, pronounced *rho*) is calculated using ranks. This happens when the scores are in the form of ranks, or when exam scores are converted to ranks first. However, Spearman's correlation is not interpreted like Pearson's correlation in terms of overlap or coefficient of determination. Spearman's correlation only shows how similar two sets of ranks are.

Both r and ρ are assumed to have linear relationship for the two variables correlated. If linearity is not satisfied, the correlations do not apply.

Reliability: Exam scores must show a certain degree of reliability before they are valid and can be sued for making decisions. The Cronbach's alpha coefficient (α) and its variants are calculated for verification.

Cronbach's alpha coefficient: The α-coefficient indicates the extent to which an exam is *internally consistent*, that is to say the items making up the exam measure highly similar ability (or knowledge).

Imagine that we have a 30-item exam for assessing language proficiency, be it for English or a Mother Tongue Language. Naturally, the items deal with different aspects or ability of that language. We can calculate the correlation coefficients for all pairs of items (i.e., Items 1–2, Items 1–3,... Items 29–30) and this results in 435 different r's (!). We then calculate the average (mean) of these large number of r's. The result is the Cronbach's α-coefficient. [Now, you appreciate the usefulness of the computer; my experience of calculating one r manually took me about 20 minutes.]

Since items making up an exam are usually measuring the same kind of ability (e.g., Mathematics) or knowledge (e.g., Science), the items are usually positively correlated and the r's will usually be positive, and the resultant α-coefficient is usually positive. The α-coefficient may be low (say, $\alpha = 0.4$) or high (say, $\alpha = 0.8$).

How high should α-coefficient be to be taken as satisfactory? This depends on the context. For research purposes, $\alpha = 0.7$ is the minimum expected, but for making decision on individual students (and all exams do!) $\alpha = 0.9$ is expected (a standard set by the American Psychological Association for educational and psychological standardized tests).

However, $\alpha = 0.9$ may not be attainable for classroom tests made by teachers who, hopefully, make good use of the information to guide teaching and modification to curriculum. For such purposes, a lower $\alpha = 0.7$ may be fine, as teaching and curriculum modification are, in a sense, research.

It is also noteworthy that research is affected by many factors, some of which are not within the control of teachers. Two conditions within the teachers' control are test length and item formats. Firstly, when items are of good qualities (e.g., F-indices and D-indices), the longer the test the better its reliability; this means teachers need to use as many items as practically possible to ensure higher degree of reliability, especially if the exam is for assessment of learning or summative assessment. Secondly, when an exam consists of many different item formats, the abilities assessed are different in nature, and this is likely to yield lower reliability. For this reason, it is advisable to keep the different item formats within an exam as low as possible.

Kuder-Richardson Reliability: Before the appearance of Cronbach's α-coefficient, Kuder-Richardson reliability was popular in educational (and psychological) measurement. It was later realized that when items are dichotomously scored ($1 = $ right and $0 = $ Wrong), Cronbach's α-coefficient and Kuder-Richardson reliability have the same value. Then, Kuder-Richardson reliability is a specific case of Cronbach's α-coefficient. In the school context, many test items take the form of dichotomy in scoring, either of the two approaches is equally acceptable.

In the above discussion, Kuder-Richardson reliability uses the Kuder-Richardson 20 Formula, which used the students' actual responses for calculation. However, as an estimate of the Kuder-Richardson 20 reliability, there is the Kuder-Richardson 21 Formula which needs only the number of item, the mean, and the variance (i.e., the square of standard deviation).

Standardization: When students take an exam, they are awarded a score (mark) according to their responses. This score is a *raw score* because it is unprocessed or untreated. Raw scores have been used to report student achievement and has been interpreted literarily at its face value, with no reference to any other relevant information.

For example, a raw score of 50 for a language exam may be interpreted as a 'pass', with the tacit assumption of a full-mark of 100 and 50% is, by Singapore convention, the cut-score (passing mark). For another example, when Adrian gets 70 for English and 60 for Mathematics, he is likely to be seen as passing both exams but better in English than in Mathematics. Such interpretation is rather common among teachers, school leaders, and parents. It may be correct and it may not be: what if the full-mark for English is 100 but that for Mathematics is 60? It is risky to interpret exam results without reference to other relevant information. This is where standardization helps and, in fact, is needed.

As discussed earlier, the two most important statistical characteristics of a set of exam results is the mean and the SD. Recall that the mean indicates the general level of performance — how well the students have done for the exam, and the SD shows how different the students are on the text — the heterogeneity among the students.

z-score: Armed with these statistical information, instead of reporting a student's performance in terms of his raw score, which has doubtful and uncertain meanings, he can be reported as *above, at,* or *below* the mean, that is, his deviation from the mean (which indicates the performance of the group as a whole. However, as such description is not specific enough to be useful, he can be reported as how much his deviation is from the mean in terms of SD. If the mean is taken to be the centre (0) and he scores exactly that score (mean, he is not deviating from the mean and gets a standardized score of zero (0), and since he has no deviation, this standardized score (z-score) is 0.00.

His classmate, say Albert, has done better than he did, and the deviation happens to be equal to the SD, so Albert will have a z-score of 1.00. Another classmate Alfred gets a poorer score and this happens to be exactly one SD below the mean, his z-score is −1.00.

With reference to the normal curve, a z-score of 0.00 means the students perform just as well as a typical student of the group has done — average. A $z = 1.00$ indicates that the student is standing at the 68th percentile and is better than 68 percent of his peers. Likewise, a z-score = −1.00 means the student is at the 16th percentile and is better than only 16 percent of his peers. In short, a standard score (z) indicates the relative position of a student among his peers. Other z-scores are interpreted accordingly.

The z-score is calculated using the formula:

$$z\text{-score} = (\text{Score} - \text{Mean})/\text{SD}$$

T-score: The z-score with decimal and negative sign is inconvenient to use. Clerical carelessness with decimal and negative sign can create havoc. Miscopying a negative sign turn a poor student into an achieving one (on paper, of course). A negative score may lead to the misinterpretation that the student owes the teacher something, since negative figures usually mean deficits. To avoid such problems, measurement experts have come up with the T-score, taking the advantages of the z-score and avoid its probable mistakes.

T-transformation is as very simple statistical operation using the formula:

$$\text{T-score} = 10*z\text{-score} + 50$$
$$= 10*(\text{Score} - \text{Mean})/\text{SD} + 50$$

A very important function of the T-score is that it enables "comparability" across different exams. This facilitates valid comparison across exam results of the same or different subjects. The problem of comparing scores for different exams (subjects) has been alluded to above: Adrian's 70 for English and 60 for Mathematics. If the two raw scores are transformed to T-scores, it may turn out that the English 70 is equivalent to T-score = 75 and the Mathematics 60 is equivalent to T-score = 80. In this case, it is clear that Adrian is better in Math than in English.

Another advantage of T-transformation is when scores for subjects are combined to obtain a total score and based on which the 'overall' academic performance is inferred. [This is often done in the school's report card.]

It is a well-known fact that different subject exams have different difficulties and the different sets of exam scores will have different spread as indicated by their different SDs. It is a well-known statistical fact (often overlooked) that when raw scores are combined, those scores from the distribution with wider spread (greater SD) will be automatically weighted to become more influence in the total score thus obtained. This also means the same scores (say, 65) for different subjects are not equivalent and cannot be simply equated; the score from a wider distribution is more powerful or influential in the total score; thus, 65 for English and 65 for Science are not equal in determining the final total score — if English has a wider spread (greater SD), it is a more powerful subject and may be over-riding the influence of Science which has a narrow spread (small SD) thus rendering Science non-functioning in discriminating students (and discriminating students of different ability is an important function of examinations).

Through T-transformation (or some other statistical transformation schemes; there are several commonly used ones in standardized testing), the raw scores are weighted by their SDs and the standard scores are equivalent. If two raw scores have been transformed and have the same standard score (say, T-score), they are considered as equivalent in the final overall. [Analogously, SGD 100 is not equivalent to AUD 100. We need to transform them into USD to be able to compare them correctly.]

Appendix B: Interesting and Useful Websites

The websites listed below serve two functions. First, they support the arguments made in the text. Secondly, they provide interesting and useful information in addition to those presented. Readers are urged to access these websites for more information and better understanding.

[1] *The Effects of External Rewards on Intrinsic Motivation.*
     http://www.abcbodybuilding.com/rewards.pdf

[2] *High/Scope Perry Preschool: Ypsilanti, MI.*
     http://www.aypf.org/publications/compendium/C2S45.pdf

[3] *Multiple choice questions: A literature review on the optimal number of options.*
     http://www.ncbi.nlm.nih.gov/pubmed/19004145

[4] *Testing the Test: Comparing SEMAC and Exact word Scoring on Selective Deletion Cloze.*
     http://www.nuis.ac.jp/~hadley/publication/kortesol/Hadley-Naaykens-KOTESOL.pdf

[5] *Education and Socioeconomic Status.*
     http://www.apa.org/pi/ses/resources/publications/factsheet-education.aspx

[6] *Bell Curve: Normal Curve Distribution of IQ scores.*
     http://www.assessmentpsychology.com/bellcurve.htm

[7] *An Illustration of Basic Probability: The Normal Distribution*
     http://www.ms.uky.edu/~mai/java/stat/GaltonMachine.html

[8] *A Primer on Setting Cut Scores on Tests of Educational Achievement.*
http://www.ets.org/Media/Research/pdf/Cut_Scores_Primer.pdf

[9] *Multivariate Analysis of Factors Influencing Reliability of Teacher made Tests.*
http://journals.sbmu.ac.ir/index.php/jme/article/viewFile/765/666

[10] *The Reliability of Essay Marking in High-Stakes Chinese Second Language Exams.*
http://findarticles.com/p/articles/mi_6934/is_2_42/ai_n28469148/

[11] *Student Characteristics and Prediction of Success in a Conventional University Mathematics Course.*
http://www.jstor.org/pss/20151745

[12] *Yerkes-Dodson Human Performance Curve*
http://sourcesofinsight.com/2008/01/14/yerkes-dodson-human-performance-curve/

[13] *The Boy who Knew Too Much: A Student Prodigy.*
http://scientific-student-prodigy.blogspot.com/2009/02/creative-children-in-classroom.html

[14] *Torrance Tests of Creative Thinking as Predictors of Personal and Public Achievement: A Fifty-Year Follow-Up*
http://www.tandfonline.com/doi/full/10.1080/10400419.2010.523393#preview

[15] *Ideational Fluency and other Characteristics of Creative Individuals.*
http://www.is.wayne.edu/drbowen/crtvyw02/Guilford.htm

[16] *Project Work.*
http://www.moe.gov.sg/education/programmes/project-work/

[17] *Project Work Grading Method Is Fair: MOE*
http://www.asiaone.com/News/Education/Story/A1Story20080425-61865.html
http://www.asiaone.com/News/Education/Story/A1Story20080425-61864.html

[18] *Ranking of Junior Colleges (JC) in Singapore.*
http://www.physics.com.sg/jcranking.htm

[19] *Cohen's kappa.*
http://en.wikipedia.org/wiki/Cohen's_kappa

[20] *Fleiss's kappa.*
http://en.wikipedia.org/wiki/Fleiss'_kappa)

[21] *Final Presentation Rubric.*
http://ed.fnal.gov/lincon/w01/projects/library/rubrics/presrubric.htm

[22] Thurlow, M., Elliott, J., & Ysseldyke, J. (2011). *Out-of-Level Testing: Pros and Cons.* National Center for Educational Outcomes, Policy Directions 9. Retrieved from
http://www.cehd.umn.edu/NCEO/OnlinePubs/Policy9.htm/

www.ingramcontent.com/pod-product-compliance
Lightning Source LLC
Chambersburg PA
CBHW071744270326
41928CB00013B/2797